Teaching Calculation:
Audit and Test

Teaching Calculation: Audit and Test

Richard English

Series editor: Alice Hansen

Los Angeles | London | New Delhi
Singapore | Washington DC

Learning Matters
An imprint of SAGE Publications Ltd
1 Oliver's Yard
55 City Road
London EC1Y 1SP

SAGE Publications Inc.
2455 Teller Road
Thousand Oaks, California 91320

SAGE Publications India Pvt Ltd
B 1/I 1 Mohan Cooperative Industrial Area
Mathura Road
New Delhi 110 044

SAGE Publications Asia-Pacific Pte Ltd
3 Church Street
#10-04 Samsung Hub
Singapore 049483

Editor: Amy Thornton
Development editor: Jennifer Clark
Production controller: Chris Marke
Project management: Deer Park Productions, Tavistock, Devon, England
Marketing Manager: Catherine Slinn
Cover design: Wendy Scott
Typeset by: C&M Digitals (P) Ltd, Chennai, India
Printed in Great Britain by Henry Ling Limited at The Dorset Press, Dorchester, DT1 1HD

First published by Learning Matters SAGE 2013

Library of Congress Control Number: 2013946209

British Library Cataloguing in Publication data

A catalogue record for this book is available from the British Library

MIX
Paper from
responsible sources
FSC™ C013985
www.fsc.org

ISBN: 978-1-4462-7276-3
ISBN: 978-1-4462-7277-0 (pbk)

Contents

Introduction   vi

1   Developing a feel for number   1

2   Mental calculation and the recall of   10
     number facts

3   The development of pencil-and-paper   23
     calculation

4   Traditional pencil-and-paper calculation   39

5   Calculating with fractions, decimals,   55
     percentages and ratios

6   Calculation using technology   69

     Appendix 1   79

     Appendix 2   80

     *Appendix 3: final summary audit/test: 100 questions
     for you to try*   81

     Appendix 4: final summary audit/test: answers   85

Introduction

It is crucially important that children leave primary school with high levels of arithmetical competence and so this places immense pressure on those who have to equip children with the necessary skills. Teachers must therefore possess excellent arithmetical skills themselves, as well as the associated pedagogical knowledge.

This book has been designed to accompany *Teaching Arithmetic in Primary Schools* in such a way that the two publications complement one another. This audit book enables you to assess your arithmetical knowledge, skills and understanding, thus enabling you to identify those areas that require further attention, whereas the original book provides a more detailed consideration of all aspects of teaching calculation. Together, the two books provide a comprehensive coverage of this vitally important aspect of primary mathematics.

The chapters in this audit book correspond to those in the original and so cover all aspects of calculation, from the recall of number facts and mental skills through to informal and formal pencil-and-paper methods. There are also chapters in both books dedicated to fractions, decimals, percentages and ratios, and the use of technology in the teaching of calculation.

Chapter structure

Each chapter starts by identifying the learning outcomes so that you can see precisely which aspects of your subject and pedagogical knowledge are going to be addressed. This will enable you to prioritise those chapters that need to be consulted first, whilst others can be left until later.

The introduction to each chapter raises some key issues through a series of 'agree/disagree' statements for you to consider. You will find a discussion of these issues at the end of each chapter.

The sections that follow present a large number of questions for you to attempt, so as to establish your current levels of knowledge, skills and understanding in relation to both mathematical content and pedagogy. Again, you will find the answers at the end of each chapter, together with working out and explanatory notes that will enable you to identify where you may have gone wrong and what might be a better approach. This audit book does not provide as much detail and explanation as the original book but, nevertheless, provides enough feedback to help you to decide whether or not you need to explore each topic further.

If the initial audit indicates that you do need to spend more time on a particular aspect of calculation, the 'What to do next?' section provides some ideas as to what the next steps might be. This section identifies chapters of other subject knowledge books that you could consult and also identifies ways in which you can develop your knowledge of pedagogy and the curriculum through school-based activities. Finally, there is a 'Recommended reading' section which provides further details of the sources specifically mentioned in the previous section, together with additional ones that are also worth considering.

How to use this book

This book has been designed to be used flexibly according to your own particular circumstances and needs. For example, there are several ways in which you could use the book in terms of timing, as indicated by the possibilities below. You could:

- work through the whole book prior to starting your training, so that you know in advance your current levels of competence and therefore what remedial action needs to be taken;

- consult particular sections of the book during your training according to the current topics that are being covered by your mathematics tutors and mentors;

- use the book immediately before and during a teaching placement so as to ensure that your subject and pedagogical knowledge are at a sufficiently high level in order to teach particular aspects of calculation;

- revisit some or all of the book at the end of your initial training to help you identify subject-specific targets for your first year of teaching, which in turn can feed into a programme of professional development for mathematics.

There is also flexibility in terms of who actually uses the materials in this book, as indicated by these possibilities:

- You could use the book on your own, working independently throughout.

- You could work through some or all of the book with a fellow-trainee or a small group of fellow-trainees, thus encouraging discussion and debate about the methods presented and the issues raised.

- Mathematics tutors and mentors could utilise some of the materials presented in this book when working with groups of trainees as part of their training.

- Although primarily aimed at trainees, the book is also relevant to experienced teachers who want to audit and develop their subject knowledge.

A final word of encouragement

If you are a trainee about to embark on your training it is possible that this audit book will identify large gaps in your subject and pedagogical knowledge, but there is no need to panic or consider throwing in the towel just yet! Your tutors and mentors will provide you with plenty of training, advice and support throughout the initial stages of your professional development. However, you must also be prepared to take ownership of this yourself and devote whatever time is necessary to equip yourself appropriately to teach calculation in primary schools.

Richard English

References

English, R. (2013) *Teaching Arithmetic in Primary Schools*. London: Learning Matters/ SAGE.

1 Developing a feel for number

Learning outcomes

This chapter will help you to:

- audit the extent to which you possess the essential knowledge and understanding that underpin calculation;
- develop a better understanding of numbers and the number system;
- identify resources that will help you to develop a feel for number.

Introduction

Before exploring the subject of calculation itself, it is important to ensure that you have a sound understanding of the numbers you will be working with and the fascinating ways in which they relate to one another. The aim of this chapter is therefore to establish the extent to which you possess a good 'feel for number' because this is an essential prerequisite for your own competence with calculation and is something that you should be seeking to develop amongst the children you teach.

After attempting the questions in each section below, check your responses with those that can be found at the end of this chapter.

Section 1: understanding numbers – multiples, factors and primes

1. Write down the first few multiples of 5. What do you notice about them? Write down anything at all that you think is of interest. How do they relate to the multiples of 10?

2. Write down the first few multiples of 3. What do you notice about them? Write down anything at all that you think is of interest. How do the multiples of 3 relate to the multiples of other numbers?

3. Write down the first few multiples of 4. What do you notice about them? Write down anything at all that you think is of interest. How do the multiples of 4 relate to the multiples of other numbers?

4. Write down the first few multiples of 9. What do you notice about them? Write down anything at all that you think is of interest. Are there any interesting patterns in the digits?

5. Write down all the factors of 24.

6. Write down all the factors of 35.

7. When listing factors it is often helpful to look for them in pairs (called 'factor pairs'). For example when listing the factors of 28 you might start with 1 and 28 (because $1 \times 28 = 28$), followed by 2 and 14 (because $2 \times 14 = 28$), and so on. So if factors occur in pairs, does this mean that a number always has an even number of factors? Can you find a number which has an odd number of factors?

8. How can you tell, without carrying out any calculations, that 2, 4, 5, 6, 8 and 10 are not factors of 657?

9. Does 657 have any other factors apart from 1 and 657? Do you know any quick ways of checking?

10. Can you check quickly to see if 85,632 is divisible by 4? Which part of the number do you need to focus on? Why?

11. Is 85,632 divisible by 3? Do you know a quick way of checking?

12. Is 85,632 divisible by 6? Do you know a quick way of checking?

13. Is 547,856 divisible by 8? Do you know a quick way of checking?

14. What is the definition of a prime number? What is the first prime number?

Section 2: understanding calculation
Agree/disagree

Read the following statements and decide whether you agree or disagree with each one. Use examples to explain your decisions. Then compare your thoughts with the notes provided at the end of the chapter.

15. Subtraction always involves 'taking away' – i.e. the physical removal of objects.

16. Division always involves sharing a quantity equally into a number of parts.

17. When you add something to a number, the answer is always going to be more than the original number.

18. When you subtract something from a number, the answer is always going to be less than the original number.

19. When a number is multiplied by something, the answer is always going to be more than the original number.

20. When a number is divided by something, the answer is always going to be less than the original number.

More questions for you to try

21. Without actually calculating 283×38 decide which of the following is the correct answer: (a) 10,753; (b) 10,754; (c) 10,755. How do you know?

22. Without actually calculating 137×49 decide which of the following is the correct answer: (a) 6712; (b) 6713; (c) 6714. How do you know?

23. Without actually calculating 179×23 decide which of the following is the correct answer: (a) 4113; (b) 4115; (c) 4117. How do you know?

24. Why do $258 + 137$ and $260 + 135$ give the same answer?

25. Why do $376 - 268$ and $378 - 270$ give the same answer?

26. Why do 144×3 and 72×6 give the same answer?

27. Why do $450 \div 36$ and $150 \div 12$ and $75 \div 6$ and $25 \div 2$ all give the same answer?

28. What is the commutative law? Give examples to illustrate your answer.

29. What is the associative law? Give examples to illustrate your answer.

30. What is the distributive law? Give examples to illustrate your answer.

What to do next?

Developing your own subject knowledge

To develop your understanding of numbers and the number system, it is recommended that you consult the following sources:

- *Mathematics Explained for Primary Teachers*, Chapter 6 ('Number and place value') and Chapter 14 ('Multiples, factors, primes').

- *Primary Mathematics: Teaching Theory and Practice*, Chapter 7 ('Number').

- *Teaching Arithmetic in Primary Schools*, pages 36–37 ('Understanding the number system').

- *Understanding and Teaching Primary Mathematics*, Chapter 4 ('Counting and understanding number').

Also find out about other special sets of numbers that feature in the mathematics curriculum, such as square numbers, triangular numbers, the Fibonacci sequence, Pascal's triangle, the golden ratio, and so on. Investigate some of the patterns and relationships that exist within these numbers. For example, have a look at the differences between consecutive square numbers. What do you notice? Add any two consecutive triangular numbers. What do you notice? Write down the sum of each horizontal row of numbers in Pascal's triangle. What do you notice? These are just a few examples of the fascinating patterns and relationships that can be explored within our number system. Having an awareness of them, or at least possessing the capacity to investigate them, will contribute to your overall 'feel for number' and therefore your ability to calculate effectively.

To find out more about the commutative, associative and distributive laws, it is recommended that you read the following:

- *Primary Mathematics: Knowledge and Understanding*, pages 18–19 ('The laws of arithmetic').

- *Teaching Arithmetic in Primary Schools*, pages 33–36 ('The laws of arithmetic').

Developing your knowledge of the curriculum

Read the National Curriculum programmes of study for mathematics and identify those aspects which focus on children's understanding of the number system. When you have identified these aspects, discuss them with staff in your placement schools and find out how teachers address them. Also have a look at the commercial schemes, resource books, software and other materials that are used by schools to support these aspects of the mathematics curriculum.

Recommended reading

Cotton, T. (2010) *Understanding and Teaching Primary Mathematics*. Harlow: Pearson Education.

English, R. (2013) *Teaching Arithmetic in Primary Schools*. London: Learning Matters/ SAGE.

Haylock, D. (2010) *Mathematics Explained for Primary Teachers* (4th edn). London: SAGE.

Mooney, C., Briggs, M., Fletcher, M., Hansen, A. and McCullouch, J. (2012) *Primary Mathematics: Teaching Theory and Practice* (6th edn). London: Learning Matters/SAGE.

Mooney, C., Ferrie, L., Fox, S., Hansen, A. and Wrathmell, R. (2012) *Primary Mathematics: Knowledge and Understanding* (6th edn). London: Learning Matters/ SAGE.

Answers

Section 1: understanding numbers – multiples, factors and primes

1. Here are some of the things you may have noted about the multiples of 5:

- The final digit is always 5 or 0.

- The final digits alternate between being 5 and 0.

- They alternate between being odd and even.

- The even multiples of 5 are multiples of 10.

2. Here are some of the things you may have noted about the multiples of 3:

   - They alternate between being odd and even.

   - The even multiples of 3 are multiples of 6.

   - Some of the multiples of 3 are multiples of 9 (every 3rd one).

3. Here are some of the things you may have noted about the multiples of 4:

   - They are all even.

   - Alternate multiples of 4 are multiples of 8.

4. Here are some of the things you may have noted about the multiples of 9:

   - They alternate between being odd and even.

   - The 10s digit increases by 1 as the 1s digit decreases by 1.

   - The digit sum is always 9. For example 27 (2 + 7 = 9), 36 (3 + 6 = 9), 99 (9 + 9 = 18 and 1 + 8 = 9)

   - They are all multiples of 3.

5. The factors of 24 are 1, 2, 3, 4, 6, 8, 12 and 24.

6. The factors of 35 are 1, 5, 7 and 35.

7. Not all numbers have an even number of factors. An example is 25 (factors are 1, 5 and 25 – i.e. 3 in total). Another example is 36 (factors are 1, 2, 3, 4, 6, 9, 12, 18 and 36 – i.e. 9 in total). Another is 49 (factors are 1, 7 and 49 – i.e. 3 in total). Have you spotted what these numbers have in common? They are square numbers. Square numbers are the only numbers that have an odd number of factors because one of the 'factors pairs' is a number which pairs with itself.

8. 657 is not divisible by 2, 4, 6, 8 or 10 because it is not an even number (all multiples of an even number are even); 657 is not divisible by 5 because the final digit is not a 5 or 0.

9. 657 is divisible by 9 because if you add the digits, you get 9:

   $$6 + 5 + 7 = 18$$

   $$1 + 8 = 9$$

This test can be applied to any number to check for divisibility by 9. 657 is also divisible by 3 because all multiples of 9 are multiples of 3 or, put another way, if 9 is a factor of 657, then 3 must also be a factor.

10. 85,632 is divisible by 4 because the 2-digit number at the end (32) is divisible by 4. You don't need to consider the other digits because 100 is divisible by 4 and therefore 600 must be divisible by 4, as indeed are 5600 and 85,600. So just look at the 2-digit number at the end. This test for divisibility by 4 can be applied to any number.

11. 85,632 is divisible by 3 because if you add the digits you get 6:

$$8 + 5 + 6 + 3 + 2 = 24$$

$$2 + 4 = 6$$

    If you get 3, 6 or 9 then the original number is divisible by 3. This test for divisibility by 3 can be applied to any number.

12. Make use of what you learned from question 2 above – i.e. multiples of 6 are even and are multiples of 3. So if a number is even (just look at the final digit) and it is also a multiple of 3 (use the test introduced in question 11 above) then it must be a multiple of 6. 85,632 is even and it is divisible by 3 and so must be divisible by 6.

13. 547,856 is divisible by 8 because the 3-digit number at the end (856) is divisible by 8. You don't need to consider the other digits because 1000 is divisible by 8 and therefore 7000 must be divisible by 8, as indeed are 47,000 and 547,000. So just look at the 3-digit number at the end. This test for divisibility by 8 can be applied to any number.

14. A common definition of a prime number is 'A number which is only divisible by itself and 1'. The problem with this definition is that it results in confusion regarding whether or not 1 is a prime number. 1 is divisible by itself and it is divisible by 1, and so many people conclude that 1 is a prime number. However, this is not correct because the first prime number is in fact 2. A better definition of a prime number, which removes any confusion, is 'A number with exactly 2 factors'.

Section 2: understanding calculation

15. Children are often introduced to subtraction as 'taking away' objects, but it is not helpful to always think of subtraction in this way. Sometimes subtraction relates to the difference between two quantities or measures – for example, the difference between two test scores, or the difference between two people's heights. In such cases we focus on the gap between the two numbers and find the answer by counting back or counting forwards from one to the other. There is no 'taking away' as such.

16. Children's first encounters with division are usually in the context of sharing, whereby a set of objects is shared equally between a group of children, by dealing

the objects out like a pack of cards: 'One for you, one for you, one for me...'. However, once an understanding of division has been established, most people think of it as grouping. So, for example, when faced with a calculation such as 98 ÷ 7 it is viewed in terms of 'How many lots of 7 can I get from 98' and so can be tackled by repeatedly subtracting lots of 7 from 98. This forms the basis of the 'chunking' method of division.

17. If you add a positive number, the answer will be more than the original number. However, if you add a negative number the answer will be less than the original. To make this clearer let's think in terms of money. If you've got £20 and you are given another £5 then you will have £25, as indicated by the following number sentence: 20 + 5 = 25. However, if you have £20, but then someone presents you with a previously written 'IOU' for £5 then you will have only £15, as indicated by the following number sentence: 20 + -5 = 15.

18. If you subtract a positive number, the answer will be less than the original number. However, if you subtract a negative number, the answer will be more than the original number. One way of explaining this is to refer back to the 'IOU' in question 17 above. If someone takes the £5 IOU away from you, you will be £5 better off, as indicated by the following number sentence: 15 – -5 = 20. So when you subtract a negative number it is equivalent to adding the positive version. You may recall being told as a child that 'A minus and a minus makes a plus', but without any explanation as to why this is so, when in fact it is not particularly difficult to comprehend. One possibility is to look at the patterns in number sentences which subtract decreasing amounts, as shown below:

$$5 - 2 = 3$$
$$5 - 1 = 4$$
$$5 - 0 = 5$$
$$5 - -1 = 6$$
$$5 - -2 = 7$$

There are clear patterns as you look down each column of numbers and these demonstrate that subtracting a negative number is equivalent to adding the positive version.

Another way of explaining this is to think of subtraction as being the difference between two numbers on a number line. In the case of the final subtraction above, the answer is the gap between 5 and −2 on a number line, which is 7. In the case of 15 and −5 the gap is 20, which is the answer provided above.

19. A common misconception amongst children is that multiplication always makes things bigger, but this is not the case if the multiplier is between 0 and 1, as illustrated by the following examples:

$8 \times 0.5 = 4$, i.e. half of 8

$10 \times 0.1 = 1$, i.e. one-tenth of 10

$12 \times 0.25 = 3$, i.e. one-quarter of 12

20. Another common misconception is that division always makes things smaller, but this is not the case if the divisor is between 0 and 1, as illustrated by the following examples:

$3 \div 0.5 = 6$, i.e. how many 0.5s (halves) are there in 6?

$1.5 \div 0.1 = 15$, i.e. how many 0.1s (tenths) are there in 1.5?

$3 \div 0.25 = 12$, i.e. how many 0.25s (quarters) are there in 3?

21. The answer is (b) 10,754. One quick way of establishing this is to make use of the fact that an odd number multiplied by an even number always gives an even answer. Only one of the three possibilities is even.

22. The answer is (b) 6713. One quick way of establishing this is to make use of the fact that an odd number multiplied by another odd number always gives an odd answer. Only one of the three possibilities is odd.

23. Based on the point raised in question 22 above (ODD × ODD – ODD), the answer will be an odd number. However, all three options are odd, so this strategy is of no use on this occasion. Another possibility is to multiply the final digits in the two numbers – i.e. $9 \times 3 = 27$. This indicates that the final digit in the answer will be 7, so the correct option is (c) 4117. This strategy could also have been used to answer questions 21 and 22.

24. When carrying out an addition, you can add an amount to one of the numbers and subtract the same amount from one of the others, without it affecting the final answer. This strategy can be used to simplify the calculation, as in the example provided – i.e. most people would consider $260 + 135$ to be an easier calculation than $258 + 137$. Both produce the same answer: 395.

25. When carrying out a subtraction (think in terms of difference), if you add or subtract the same amount to both numbers, the difference between them remains the same. This strategy can be used to simplify the calculation, as in the example provided – i.e. most people would consider $378 - 270$ to be an easier calculation than $376 - 268$. Both produce the same answer: 108.

26. When carrying out a multiplication, you can multiply one of the numbers by a particular amount and divide the other number by the same amount, without it affecting the final answer. This strategy can be used to produce an equivalent calculation. For example, from the original multiplication 144 has been divided by 2, and 3 has been multiplied by 2, to produce 72×6, which some people might consider to be an easier calculation. Both produce the same answer: 432.

27. When carrying out a division, if you divide both numbers by the same amount, this does not affect the final answer. This strategy can be used to produce an equivalent calculation which is much simpler than the original. For example, in the original division 450 and 36 have both been divided by 3, then by 2 and then by 3, to give 25 and 2. This is very similar to the notion of 'cancelling down' fractions by dividing the numerator and denominator by the same amount.

In a similar fashion you can multiply both numbers by the same amount to produce an equivalent, but simpler, calculation, as illustrated by the example below:

$3.5 \div 1.25 =$ multiply both numbers by 4

$14 \div 5 =$ to produce an easier calculation

28. The commutative law indicates whether or not the order in which two numbers and one mathematical operation are combined affects the answer:

addition is commutative because $2 + 3 = 3 + 2$

multiplication is commutative because $4 \times 5 = 5 \times 4$

Subtraction and division are not commutative.

29. The associative law indicates whether or not the order in which three or more numbers and one or more mathematical operations are combined affects the answer. Addition is associative because when calculating $2 + 3 + 4$ the numbers can be added in the order they appear, or alternatively $3 + 4$ can be calculated first and the answer added to the 2. Brackets can be used to indicate which parts of a calculation should be carried out first. So addition is associative because:

$$(2 + 3) + 4 = 2 + (3 + 4)$$

and multiplication is associative because

$$(2 \times 3) \times 4 = 2 \times (3 \times 4)$$

but subtraction is not associative because

$$(5 - 3) - 1 \neq 5 - (3 - 1)$$

30. The distributive law indicates whether or not one mathematical operation can be distributed across another. Multiplication can be distributed over addition because:

$$5 \times 13 = 5 \times (10 + 3) = 5 \times 10 + 5 \times 3$$

In the above example multiplication by 5 has been distributed over the addition of 10 and 3.

2 Mental calculation and the recall of number facts

Learning outcomes

This chapter will help you to:

- ensure that you understand the nature and importance of mental calculation and the recall of number facts;
- audit your ability to recall number facts quickly;
- audit your mental calculation skills;
- audit your ability to apply mental skills in a range of mathematical contexts;
- identify strategies and resources to develop efficient mental calculation skills and the ability to recall number facts quickly.

Introduction

Before auditing your ability to recall number facts and your mental calculation skills, let us first consider the nature and importance of these two areas of mathematical capability.

Agree/disagree

Read the following statements and decide whether you agree or disagree with each one. Then compare your thoughts with the notes provided at the end of the chapter.

1. Mental calculation and recalling number facts mean the same thing.

2. Mental calculation skills do not need to be taught because they are very personal to each individual and children are capable of developing these for themselves.

3. Mental practice should take place only during the first few minutes of mathematics lessons.

4. Mental calculation is only relevant to children in KS1 and lower KS2.

5. In terms of learning multiplication facts, children should not be expected to recall anything beyond 12×12.

6. Mental calculation means that children write nothing down.

7. Once children have been introduced to written methods of calculation, they don't need to spend time on mental methods.

Section 1: how good are you at recalling number facts?

8.   Appendix 1 provides three sets of 25 questions related to addition and subtraction facts up to 20 (a National Curriculum requirement for children in Year 2). Test yourself by jotting down the answers to all the questions in set 1 and doing it against the clock. Make a note of your time. You will find the answers on page 17. You should be aiming for a near-perfect score and a time under 1 minute (that's about 2 seconds per question).

9.   Appendix 2 provides three sets of 25 multiplication and division facts questions based on multiplication facts up to 12×12 (a National Curriculum requirement for children in Year 4). Test yourself by jotting down the answers to all the questions in set 1 and doing it against the clock. Make a note of your time. You will find the answers on page 18. You should be aiming for a near-perfect score and a time under 1 minute (that's about 2 seconds per question).

If the questions above reveal that you need to improve your own recall of number facts, read the 'What to do next?' and 'Recommended reading' sections towards the end of this chapter. These will provide you with strategies to improve your recall of number facts. When you have done some reinforcement work on this, try doing the tests again. Follow-up tests can be found in Appendices 1 and 2. As with the original tests, you should be aiming for a near-perfect score and a time under 1 minute.

Section 2: how efficient are your mental calculation skills?

Mentally calculate the answer to each of the following questions. You should write down nothing apart from the answer. After answering each one make a brief note of how you tackled it. When you have answered each question and made brief notes on your methods, compare them with those provided at the end of the chapter.

10. $63 + 24$

11. $54 + 39$

12. $47 + 35 + 23$

13. $198 + 86$

14. $96 - 54$

15. $75 - 49$

16. $253 - 248$

17. $163 - 16 - 44$

18. $56 - 39 + 24$

19. $1 + 2 + 3 + 4 + 5 + 6 + 7 + 8 + 9 + 10$

20. 14×6

21. 7×19

22. 300×8

23. 4×27

24. 600×40

25. 34×5

26. $126 \div 3$

27. $375 \div 25$

28. $380 \div 5$

29. $284 \div 4$

30. $270 \div 30$

Section 3: applying your mental calculation skills

The previous two sections should have helped you to identify your current levels of competence with regard to your mental calculation skills and your ability to recall number facts. However, there is little point in being good at calculation if you cannot utilise it effectively, so this section will audit your ability to apply your mental skills in a range of contexts.

The contexts provided in the questions below represent only a small subset of the many possibilities that you and the children you teach will encounter and so they should be seen as just examples rather than an exhaustive list.

Mentally calculate the answer to each of the following questions. As before, you should write down nothing apart from the answer. When you have completed all the questions, compare your answers with those provided at the end of the chapter.

31. The admission charge for a theme park is £18 for adults and £7 for children. What is the total cost for a party comprising 3 adults and 3 children?

32. A rectangular sports hall is 29 metres long and 15 metres wide. What is its perimeter in metres?

33. What is the area of the sports hall described above in square metres?

34. 339 children are going on a school trip. Each coach will seat 68 children. How many coaches are needed?

35. In the six mental recall tests presented in section 1 above a trainee teacher scored 22, 24, 24, 23, 21 and 24. What is his mean score?

36. Two of the internal angles in a triangle are 39 degrees and 86 degrees. What is the size of the third angle in degrees?

37. A cake recipe requires 6 ounces of sugar. If an ounce is equivalent to 28 grams, how many grams of sugar are required?

38. A bag of sugar weighs 500 grams. What is the weight of the bag in ounces, to the nearest ounce, based on the same conversion presented above?

39. If 5 miles is approximately 8 kilometres, how many kilometres is 75 miles?

40. Using the same conversion presented above, how many miles is 400 kilometres?

What to do next?

Developing your own subject knowledge: recalling number facts

To develop your knowledge, skills and understanding in relation to the recall of number facts it is recommended that you read *Teaching Arithmetic in Primary Schools*, Chapter 2 ('The rapid recall of number facts'). This chapter provides:

- a detailed discussion of the distinction between recalling known facts and mental calculation;

- practical advice on what children need to be able to do and the best ways of achieving this;

- suggestions and activities to develop your own ability to recall number facts;

- research summaries and case studies relating to the recall of number facts.

Other sources that you might like to consult include:

- *Primary Mathematics: teaching theory and practice*, Chapter 8 ('Calculation'), particularly the section on 'Mental recall and mental calculation'.

- *Understanding and Teaching Primary Mathematics*, Chapter 5 ('Knowing and using number facts').

If your own recall of number facts still needs to be improved, even after doing the six tests in Section 1 above, you can work on this with another trainee. Each should draw up a list of questions, pitched at a similar level of difficulty to the ones in Section 1, and fire these at one another. It really is a simple case of 'practice makes perfect'.

Also make use of online resources, computer software and mobile/tablet apps that provide quick-fire practice of number facts. There is no shortage of these sorts of 'drill and skill' resources, freely available via the internet.

Developing your own subject knowledge: efficient mental calculation

To develop your knowledge, skills and understanding in relation to mental calculation it is recommended that you read *Teaching Arithmetic in Primary Schools*, Chapter 3 ('Mental arithmetic'). This chapter provides:

- a discussion of the status and importance of mental calculation;

- a detailed consideration of the principles, laws and concepts that underpin mental methods;

- numerous activities and worked examples which illustrate a wide range of mental calculation techniques;

- research summaries and case studies which highlight key issues relating to mental calculation.

Another source that you might like to consult is *Mathematics Explained for Primary Teachers*, Chapter 8 ('Mental strategies for addition and subtraction') and Chapter 11 ('Mental strategies for multiplication and addition').

If, having worked through all the questions in Sections 2 and 3 above, you still feel that you are not confident in using efficient mental methods, you can continue to work on this in a number of ways, either on your own or with another trainee. Draw up a list of questions to be answered mentally, similar to those presented in Section 2. Try to choose numbers which make it fairly straightforward to identify an efficient approach – for example, based on partitioning, or near-multiples of 10, or repeated doubling, or combining numbers that go together, and so on (look back at the examples earlier in the chapter). If you and another trainee each draw up a list of questions you can fire them at one another and also explain how you tackled each one. If you prefer to work on your own, produce a long list of questions (it's easy – just reproduce the questions you have already, but with slightly altered numbers!). Cut up your sheets of paper so that each question is on a separate slip, fold them all up and pop them into a container. Then pick questions from the container at random, answering each one mentally, but also reflecting on the efficiency of the method used. You could make a point of picking one or two every day, so as to provide regular mental practice.

If the questions in Section 3 above have identified gaps in aspects of your mathematics subject knowledge relating to shape, space, measures and handling data, it is recommended that you read the relevant sections of *Primary Mathematics: Knowledge and Understanding*. Chapter 4 focuses on measures, Chapter 5 on shape and space, and Chapter 6 on handling data.

In your everyday encounters with numbers, try to mentally juggle with them. For example, in the supermarket mentally add the prices of two or more items, or work out the price difference between two items, or work out how much it would cost for 5 of them. If you see a bus passing in the street, double the route number, or multiply it by 3 or 5 or 9. You could do the same with the numbers on car registration plates, or any other numbers that you see when you're out and about, or that you come across in newspapers and magazines.

Developing your knowledge of the curriculum

Read the National Curriculum programmes of study for mathematics and identify those aspects which focus on mental calculation and the recall of number facts. Make brief notes on what is expected of children in different age groups, so that you can see the progression in the development of these skills.

Discuss your notes with staff in your placement schools and ask about the strategies that are adopted when teaching children these vital skills. Also ask staff about the paper-based materials, practical apparatus and IT resources that are used to support the development of mental calculation and the recall of number facts.

Observe lessons in your placement schools which focus on the development of children's mental calculation and the recall of number facts. Don't restrict this to the main class in which you are based; instead try to observe lessons across a range of year groups so that you can experience the various stages in the progression of skills.

Recommended reading

Cotton, T. (2010) *Understanding and Teaching Primary Mathematics*. Harlow: Pearson Education.

DfE (2010) *Teaching Children to Calculate Mentally*. London: DfE Publications.

English, R. (2013) *Teaching Arithmetic in Primary Schools*. London: Learning Matters/ SAGE.

Haylock, D. (2010) *Mathematics Explained for Primary Teachers* (4th edn). London: SAGE.

Mooney, C., Briggs, M., Fletcher, M., Hansen, A. and McCullouch, J. (2012) *Primary Mathematics: Teaching Theory and Practice* (6th edn). London: Learning Matters/SAGE.

Mooney, C., Ferrie, L., Fox, S., Hansen, A. and Wrathmell, R. (2012) *Primary Mathematics: Knowledge and Understanding* (6th edn). London: Learning Matters/SAGE.

QCA (1999) *Teaching Mental Calculation Strategies: Guidance for Teachers at Key Stages 1 and 2*. Sudbury: QCA Publications.

Answers

Introduction

1. Mental calculation and recalling number facts are not the same thing, although the boundary between them can become rather blurred. You can recall number facts instantly because they are memorised pieces of information that you know 'off by heart', in the same way that you probably know that the capital of France is Paris and that the first man to set foot on the moon was Neil Armstrong. In contrast, mental calculation involves manipulating numbers in your head to come up with answers, usually quite quickly, but not instantly.

2. Yes, the choice of mental method will depend on personal choice as well as the numbers involved, but this is not a reason for not teaching children a range of mental approaches. Many children are capable of developing their own efficient methods, with no prompting at all from the teacher, but this cannot be left to chance and so mental calculation has to be taught in a carefully planned, structured way, just like other aspects of the mathematics curriculum.

3. Since the advent of the National Numeracy Strategy in 1999, the oral-mental starter has become a popular feature at the start of many mathematics lessons. Whilst these do provide some opportunities to discuss approaches to mental calculation, they tend to be associated with the recall of number facts. The teaching of mental skills requires more than just a few minutes at the start of a lesson and so will need to feature more substantially in the mathematics curriculum. Additionally, children should encounter opportunities to practise and develop their mental skills throughout the day, across a range of curriculum subjects and in their everyday lives beyond the classroom.

4. It is true that children should be taught mental methods before they encounter written methods and so the former will feature strongly in KS1 and lower KS2. However, the emphasis on mental calculation should be maintained throughout KS2 and beyond, so as to encompass an increasingly broader and more challenging range of numbers, such as fractions, decimals and percentages.

5. The latest curriculum requirements state that children should learn their multiplication and division facts for multiplication tables up to 12×12, but it is likely that most children will develop a bank of memorised facts that extends beyond this. For example, some children may know that $13^2 = 169$ and $14^2 = 196$. Regular mental practice, combined with their everyday experiences of number, will result in many children's banks of memorised facts expanding beyond the minimum requirements of the National Curriculum.

6. Mental calculation implies that everything is done 'in your head' without the aid of jottings, but on many occasions the question and the answer will be written down as a number sentence. Typically these number sentences are written horizontally across the page, so as not to suggest that a written columnar method should be used.

7. As discussed in question 4 above, mental calculation should maintain its status throughout KS2 and beyond, even after written methods have been introduced. Teachers should continue to afford time to the development of mental methods so that these are always seen as the first resort when children are faced with any calculation.

Section 1: how good are you at recalling number facts?

8. Here are the answers to the addition and subtraction questions in Appendix 1:

Set 1		Set 2		Set 3	
1.	10	1.	15	1.	13
2.	8	2.	28	2.	10
3.	13	3.	5	3.	27
4.	21	4.	110	4.	11
5.	5	5.	5	5.	22
6.	6	6.	19	6.	40
7.	11	7.	80	7.	24
8.	110	8.	21	8.	190
9.	21	9.	120	9.	300
10.	500	10.	24	10.	2
11.	5	11.	6	11.	60
12.	160	12.	11	12.	25
13.	17	13.	60	13.	26
14.	40	14.	22	14.	9
15.	9	15.	14	15.	24
16.	130	16.	190	16.	25
17.	25	17.	7	17.	8
18.	6	18.	19	18.	160
19.	130	19.	21	19.	500
20.	700	20.	8	20.	22
21.	21	21.	110	21.	7
22.	90	22.	6	22.	21
23.	7	23.	50	23.	120
24.	16	24.	900	24.	20
25.	22	25.	11	25.	21

9. Here are the answers to the multiplication and division questions in Appendix 2:

Set 1			Set 2			Set 3	
1.	88		1.	49		1.	60
2.	24		2.	20		2.	18
3.	9		3.	24		3.	11
4.	30		4.	7		4.	15
5.	84		5.	25		5.	8
6.	7		6.	27		6.	121
7.	8		7.	132		7.	24
8.	132		8.	7		8.	4
9.	4		9.	64		9.	120
10.	36		10.	55		10.	81
11.	9		11.	4		11.	5
12.	15		12.	35		12.	60
13.	70		13.	12		13.	36
14.	4		14.	8		14.	4
15.	27		15.	36		15.	66
16.	54		16.	24		16.	84
17.	6		17.	9		17.	7
18.	7		18.	42		18.	54
19.	56		19.	3		19.	35
20.	90		20.	21		20.	22
21.	3		21.	50		21.	7
22.	144		22.	8		22.	12
23.	40		23.	45		23.	40
24.	7		24.	10		24.	16
25.	6		25.	3		25.	12

Section 2: how efficient are your mental calculation skills?

For each question an efficient mental calculation method has been identified. Additionally, by way of contrast, a less efficient alternative has been provided. Use these examples to help you evaluate the efficiency of your mental calculation skills. If you are using an inefficient method, try to move towards a better alternative. The efficient suggestions are certainly not the only feasible ways of tackling these questions, but it is hoped that collectively they illustrate a range of possibilities that you should be employing yourself and also sharing with children.

10. $63 + 24$

> *Efficient*: methods based on partitioning – i.e. partition both numbers into 10s and 1s and then calculate $60 + 20 = 80$ and $3 + 4 = 7$, giving a final answer of 87.
>
> *Less efficient*: starting at 63, counting on 24 in 1s.

11. $54 + 39$

    Efficient: make use of near multiples of 10 – i.e. calculate $54 + 40 = 94$ and then subtract 1, because you have added 1 too many, giving a final answer of 93.

    Less efficient: visualising the traditional vertical written method, including the process of 'carrying'.

12. $47 + 35 + 23$

    Efficient: look for numbers that can be added quickly and carry out this part of the calculation first – i.e. calculate $47 + 23 = 70$ first and then add 35, giving a final answer of 105.

    Less efficient: adding the numbers in the order in which they appear, working from left to right.

13. $198 + 86$

    Efficient: make use of near multiples of 100 – i.e. calculate $200 + 86 = 286$ and then subtract 2, because you have added 2 too many, giving a final answer of 284.

    Less efficient: visualising the traditional vertical written method, including the process of 'carrying'.

14. $96 - 54$

    Efficient: methods based on partitioning – i.e. partition both numbers into 10s and 1s and then calculate $90 - 50 = 40$ and $6 - 4 = 2$, giving a final answer of 42.

    Less efficient: starting at 96, counting back 54 in 1s.

15. $75 - 49$

    Efficient: make use of near multiples of 10 – i.e. calculate $75 - 50 = 25$ and then add 1, because you have subtracted 1 too many, giving a final answer of 26.

    Less efficient: visualising the traditional vertical written method, including the process of 'borrowing' or 'exchanging'.

16. $253 - 248$

    Efficient: recognising that the two numbers are close to one another and also understanding that subtraction can be thought of as 'difference', therefore calculating the answer by counting on from 248 to 253, giving an answer of 5.

    Less efficient: any method that involves taking away or counting back 248, including the traditional vertical written methods.

17. $163 - 16 - 44$

    Efficient: understanding that subtracting 16 and then subtracting 44 is equivalent to subtracting the sum of these two numbers, and therefore calculating $16 + 44 = 60$ and then $163 - 60 = 103$.

    Less efficient: subtracting 16 from 163 and then subtracting 44 from the answer.

18. $56 - 39 + 24$

    Efficient: calculate $56 + 24 = 80$ first, because this can be done quickly, and then calculate $80 - 39 = 41$ by making use of near-multiples of 10.

Less efficient: carrying out the calculations in the order they appear, working from left to right.

19. $1 + 2 + 3 + 4 + 5 + 6 + 7 + 8 + 9 + 10$

Efficient: look for pairs of numbers that can be added quickly and easily – i.e. $1 + 9 = 10$, $2 + 8 = 10$, and so on. This gives four 10s, plus the 5, plus the 10 at the end, giving a final total of 55.

Less efficient: adding the numbers in the order they appear, working from left to right.

20. 14×6

Efficient: methods based on partitioning and an understanding of the distributive law – i.e. partition 14 into 10 and 4 and then calculate $10 \times 6 = 60$ and $4 \times 6 = 24$, giving a final answer of 84. Alternatively, if you know your multiplication facts up to 12×12, you can think of it as 12 lots of 6 plus 2 lots.

Less efficient: visualising the traditional written method for short multiplication, including the process of 'carrying'.

21. 7×19

Efficient: make use of near-multiples of 10 – i.e. calculate $7 \times 20 = 140$ and then subtract 7, to give 133, because you only require 19 lots of 7, not 20 lots.

Less efficient: visualising the traditional written method for short multiplication, including the process of 'carrying'.

22. 300×8

Efficient: making use of place value and the associative law by recognising that if $3 \times 8 = 24$ then $300 \times 8 = 2400$.

Less efficient: using repeated addition – i.e. $300 + 300 + 300\ldots$ and so on.

23. 4×27

Efficient: using repeated doubling – i.e. $27 \times 2 = 54$ and $54 \times 2 = 108$.

Less efficient: visualising the traditional written method for short multiplication, including the process of 'carrying'.

24. 600×40

Efficient: making use of place value and the associative law by recognising that if $6 \times 4 = 24$ then $600 \times 40 = 24,000$.

Less efficient: visualising the traditional written method for long multiplication.

25. 34×5

Efficient: recognising that multiplying by 5 is equivalent to multiplying by 10 and halving the answer, therefore calculating $34 \times 10 = 340$ and $340 \div 2 = 170$. Another way of thinking of this is that you can create an equivalent multiplication if you 'scale up' one of the numbers and 'scale down' the other number by the same amount. In this particular case you would halve the 34 and double the 5 to create 17×10 which can be worked out quickly.

Less efficient: visualising the traditional written method for short multiplication, including the process of 'carrying'.

26. $126 \div 3$

Efficient: methods based on partitioning – i.e. partition 126 into 120 and 6, and then divide each of these by 3, giving a final answer of 42.

Less efficient: visualising the traditional written method for short division.

27. $375 \div 25$

Efficient: understanding that division can be thought of as 'grouping' ('How many lots of 25 are in 375?') and recognising that there are 4 lots of 25 in each 100. So there are 16 lots of 25 in 400. 375 is 25 less than 400 so $375 \div 25 = 15$.

Less efficient: visualising the traditional written method for long division.

28. $380 \div 5$

Efficient: recognising that dividing by 5 is equivalent to dividing by 10 and doubling the answer, therefore calculating $380 \div 10 = 38$ and $38 \times 2 = 76$. Another way of thinking of this is that you can create an equivalent division if you 'scale up' both numbers by the same amount. In this particular case you would double both numbers to create $760 \div 10$ which can be worked out quickly.

Less efficient: visualising the traditional written method for short division.

29. $284 \div 4$

Efficient: using repeated halving – i.e. $284 \div 2 = 142$ and $142 \div 2 = 71$.

Less efficient: visualising the traditional written method for short division.

30. $270 \div 30$

Efficient: recognising that you can create an equivalent division if you 'cancel down' or 'scale down' both numbers by the same amount. In this particular case you would divide both numbers by 10 to create $27 \div 3$ which can be worked out quickly to give the answer 9. Another efficient method is to recognise that 10 lots of 30 is 300, so there must be 9 lots of 30 in 270 (because 270 is 30 less than 300).

Less efficient: visualising the traditional written method for long division.

Section 3: applying your mental calculation skills

For each question at least one efficient method has been identified. Study these examples carefully and use them to help you evaluate the efficiency of your own mental calculation skills. If you are still using less efficient methods, try to move towards better alternatives.

31. The admission charge for a theme park is £18 for adults and £7 for children. What is the total cost for a party comprising 3 adults and 3 children?

Efficient: work out the cost of one adult and one child (£18 + £7 = £25) and then multiply by 3 ($3 \times £25 = £75$).

32. A rectangular sports hall is 29 metres long and 15 metres wide. What is its perimeter in metres?

Efficient: use near-multiples of 10 to add one long side and one short side, to give 44, and then double this to give a final answer of 88 metres. Another efficient method is to double the 15 to give 30 and then add two more 30s for the long sides (near multiples of 10) to give 90. Finally you must subtract 2 because of the earlier rounding up, again giving a final answer of 88 metres.

33. What is the area of the sports hall described above in square metres?

    Efficient: use near-multiples of 10 to calculate 29×15 by working out $30 \times 15 = 450$ and then subtracting 15 to give a final answer of 435 square metres. Another efficient method is to calculate 10 lots of 29 (290), halve this to give 5 lots of 29 (145) and finally add the answers to give a final answer of 435 square metres (435m²).

34. 339 children are going on a school trip. Each coach will seat 68 children. How many coaches are needed?

    Efficient: 10 coaches can seat 680 children, so 5 coaches can seat 340 children. Therefore 5 coaches will be needed.

35. In the six mental recall tests presented in section 1 above a trainee teacher scored 22, 24, 24, 23, 21 and 24. What is his mean score?

    Efficient: all the scores are in the 20s, so calculate the mean of the final digits and then add this to 20 to give the overall mean. So, $2 + 4 + 4 + 3 + 1 + 4 = 18$ (add these in whatever order you want) and $18 \div 6 = 3$, so the mean score is $20 + 3 = 23$.

36. Two of the internal angles in a triangle are 39 degrees and 86 degrees. What is the size of the third angle in degrees?

    Efficient: use near-multiples of 10 to calculate $39 + 86 = 125$. The third angle is $180 - 125 = 55$ degrees.

37. A cake recipe requires 6 ounces of sugar. If an ounce is equivalent to 28 grams, how many grams of sugar are required?

    Efficient: use near-multiples of 10 to calculate 28×6 by working out $30 \times 6 = 180$ and then subtracting $2 \times 6 = 12$ to give a final answer of $180 - 12 = 168$ grams. Another possibility is to think of 28×6 as 5 lots of 28 plus 1 lot of 28. So, work out $28 \times 10 = 280$, halve the answer (140) and then add 28 to give a final answer of $140 + 28 = 168$ grams.

38. A bag of sugar weighs 500 grams. What is the weight of the bag in ounces, to the nearest ounce, based on the same conversion presented above?

    Efficient: 10 ounces is $28 \times 10 = 280$, so 20 ounces is 560. This is 60 grams more than in the bag, and 60 grams is approximately 2 ounces ($2 \times 28 = 56$ grams), so there must be approximately 18 ounces of sugar in the bag.

39. If 5 miles is approximately 8 kilometres, how kilometres is 75 miles?

    Efficient: if 5 miles is 8 kilometres, then 50 miles is 80 kilometres (multiply by 10) and 25 miles is 40 kilometres (divide by 2). Combine these to give 75 miles is 120 kilometres.

40. Using the same conversion presented above, how many miles is 400 kilometres?

    Efficient: if 5 miles is 8 kilometres, then 500 miles is 800 kilometres (multiply by 100) and so 250 miles is 400 kilometres (divide by 2).

3 The development of pencil-and-paper calculation

Learning outcomes

This chapter will help you to:

- understand the nature and importance of pencil-and-paper calculation and its relationship with mental calculation;
- audit your understanding of, and ability to use, informal pencil-and-paper calculation;
- identify strategies and resources to develop your knowledge, skills and understanding in relation to informal pencil-and-paper calculation.

Introduction

Before auditing your ability to utilise informal pencil-and-paper methods, let us first consider a few general issues in relation to this aspect of calculation.

Agree/disagree

Read the following statements and decide whether you agree or disagree with each one. Then compare your thoughts with the notes provided at the end of the chapter.

1. Children's first encounters with pencil-and-paper calculation should be 2-digit addition, set out in columns, using the traditional method which might sometimes involve 'carrying'.

2. Once children start to use pencil-and-paper methods they no longer require practical apparatus or visual aids, because everything is carried out in written format.

3. The most important feature of any written method is that it enables children to achieve correct answers to their calculations.

4. If children are dealing with big numbers they should always be encouraged to use pencil-and-paper methods.

5. Pencil-and-paper calculations and mental methods are very different and therefore require the teaching and learning of completely new skills.

Section 1: informal pencil-and-paper strategies for addition and subtraction

Answer each of the following questions and then compare your responses with those provided at the end of the chapter.

6. Think carefully and make notes/sketches to illustrate how you would use an empty number line (ENL) to model 57 + 38 to a group of children.

7. A teacher used an ENL to model the calculation 85 − 37 and so produced the working out below. Study it carefully and try to make sense of what it is showing. Make a step-by-step list of the stages the teacher worked through to calculate 85 − 37. Also think about the possible additional models and images that could be used to assist children's understanding of this method.

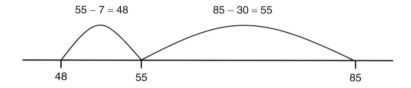

Figure 1

8. On another occasion, the same teacher used a slightly different ENL to model the same subtraction. Here is her working out. Can you see how she is explaining 85 − 37 this time? Make a list of the step-by-step stages the teacher worked through. You might be able to come up with two slightly different approaches based on this diagram. Also think about the possible additional models and images that could be used to assist children's understanding of these methods.

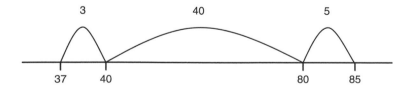

Figure 2

9. Use an ENL like the one in question 8 to calculate 726 − 359.

10. Here is the working out used by a teacher to model 57 + 38 to a group of children:

$$57 + 38 \;=\; 50 + 7 + 30 + 8$$
$$=\; 80 + 15$$
$$=\; 95$$

Are you able to make sense of this working out? What sorts of models and images could be used to support children's understanding of this method? Use the same approach yourself to calculate 345 + 482.

11. In a later lesson the teacher modelled an expanded method similar to the one in question 10 above, but this time the working was set out vertically, rather than horizontally. Try to reproduce the teacher's expanded vertical working out for 57 + 38 and for 345 + 482.

12. First read the explanation at the end of the chapter relating to question 11, so that you are aware of what the expanded vertical method for addition looks like. If instead of starting with the 10s or 100s digits, you were to start by adding the 1s (the units), would this affect the final answers? Can you see how this expanded method relates to the traditional compact method for vertical addition?

13. In a subsequent lesson, some of the children referred to in questions 7 and 8 above were ready to be introduced to a subtraction method that did not require an ENL to be drawn. Here is the teacher's working out when modelling 85 − 37:

$$
\begin{array}{ll}
37 & \\
 & (+3) \\
40 & \\
 & (+40) \\
80 & \\
 & (+5) \\
85 & \\
 & \text{(Total 48)}
\end{array}
$$

Are you able to make sense of this working out? Can you see the similarities between this working out and the ENL presented in question 7 above?

14. Use the approach presented in question 13 to calculate 726 − 359. Compare this working out with the ENL you produced for question 9 above. Are there any similarities?

15. Here is another way of working out 726 − 359:

$$
\begin{array}{r}
726 \\
-\ 359 \\
\hline
400 \\
-\ 30 \\
-3 \\
\hline
367
\end{array}
$$

Can you make sense of this method? Try to use the same approach yourself to calculate 1047 − 388.

Section 2: informal pencil-and-paper strategies for multiplication and division

Answer each of the following questions and then compare your responses with those provided at the end of the chapter.

16. Here is the working out used by a teacher to model 8×76 to a group of children:

$$
\begin{aligned}
8 \times 76 &= 8 \times 70 + 8 \times 6 \\
&= 560 + 48 \\
&= 608
\end{aligned}
$$

Are you able to make sense of this working out? Which law of arithmetic underpins this approach? What sorts of models and images could be used to support children's understanding of this method? Use the same approach yourself to calculate 7×647.

17. In a later lesson the teacher modelled an expanded method similar to the one in question 16 above, but this time the working was set out vertically, rather than horizontally. Try to reproduce the teacher's expanded vertical working out for 8×76 and for 7×647.

18. First read the explanation at the end of the chapter relating to question 17, so that you are aware of what the expanded vertical method for multiplication looks like. If instead of starting with the 10s or 100s digits, you were to start by adding the 1s (the units), would this affect the final answers? Can you see how this expanded method relates to the traditional compact method for short multiplication?

19. Used the grid method of multiplication to calculate 48×63.

20. Use the grid method of multiplication to calculate 352×89.

21. Could an expanded method, similar to those discussed in questions 16 and 17 above, have been used to calculate the answers in questions 19 and 20? If so, use this method to work out the answers.

22. Here is a child's working out for the calculation 48×63:

$$
\begin{aligned}
63 \times 100 &= 6300 \\
6300 \div 2 &= 3150 \\
3150 - 126 &= 3024
\end{aligned}
$$

Are you able to make sense of this method? Which law of arithmetic underpins this approach?

23. Here is a child's working out for the calculation $349 \div 56$:

$$
\begin{array}{cccccc}
349 & 293 & 237 & 181 & 125 & 69 \\
-\ 56 & -\ 56 & -\ 56 & -\ 56 & -\ 56 & -\ 56 \\
\hline
293 & 237 & 181 & 125 & 69 & 13
\end{array}
$$

$237 \div 56 = 6$ remainder 13.

Are you able to make sense of this working out? Use the same method to calculate $363 \div 65$, including any remainders as part of your answer. What do you see as the disadvantages and limitations of this method?

24. Another child carried out the same calculation, but saved herself a bit of work (and space), as shown below:

$349 \div 56 =$

$$
\begin{array}{r}
349 \\
-280 \quad (5 \times 56) \\
\hline
69 \\
-56 \quad (1 \times 56) \\
\hline
13
\end{array}
$$

$349 \div 56 = 6$ remainder 13.

Are you able to make sense of this working out? Use a similar approach to calculate $1132 \div 68$, including any remainders as part of your answer.

25. Read the comments at the end of the chapter relating to question 24, so that you are fully aware of the chunking method for division. Use the chunking method to calculate $873 \div 7$ and $6562 \div 43$, including any remainders as part of your answers.

What to do next?

Developing your own subject knowledge

If you feel that you need to spend more time finding out about informal pencil-and-paper methods it is recommended that you read *Teaching Arithmetic in Primary Schools*, Chapter 4 ('The development of pencil-and-paper arithmetic'). This chapter provides:

- a discussion of the progression from mental to early pencil-and-paper methods;

- detailed worked examples covering a wide range of informal pencil-and-paper approaches;

- research summaries and case studies that consider some of the key issues associated with the development of pencil-and-paper calculation.

Other sources which are worth considering include:

- *Primary Mathematics: Teaching Theory and Practice*, Chapter 8 ('Calculation'), particularly the section called 'Pencil and paper methods'.

- *Mathematics Explained for Primary Teachers*, Chapter 9 ('Written methods for addition and subtraction') and Chapter 12 ('Written methods for multiplication and division').

- *Understanding and Teaching Primary Mathematics*, Chapter 6 ('Calculating').

If you understand the various methods presented in this chapter but just need more practice then you can easily facilitate this yourself by generating random questions to answer. For example you could choose any 3 or 4-digit number, together with another 1 or 2-digit number and use these to practise an expanded method for multiplication, or the grid multiplication method, or the chunking method for division.

If any of the worked examples presented in this chapter raise other issues relating to your mathematics subject knowledge, such as the distinction between sharing and grouping when considering division, or the use of the distributive law to explain expanded methods of multiplication, refer back to Chapter 1 or the recommended reading associated with those topics.

Developing your knowledge of the curriculum

Read the National Curriculum programmes of study for mathematics and try to identify those aspects that relate to the early development of pencil-and-paper methods. The informal methods presented in this chapter may not be mentioned explicitly in the National Curriculum, but there may be extracts which could be interpreted as being relevant.

Of more direct relevance are the mathematics schemes of work devised by the schools in which you work. These are likely to provide more detail than the broad outline in the National Curriculum. Read your school's mathematics documentation to see how pencil-and-paper methods are introduced and the stages that children are expected to pass through. Speak to the person responsible for mathematics in your school and ask about the teaching of the methods presented in this chapter. Find out when the teaching of these methods is going to be taking place and make arrangements to observe this and to be directly involved in supporting the children.

Recommended reading

Cotton, T. (2010) *Understanding and Teaching Primary Mathematics*. Harlow: Pearson Education.

English, R. (2013) *Teaching Arithmetic in Primary Schools*. London: Learning Matters/ SAGE.

Haylock, D. (2010) *Mathematics Explained for Primary Teachers* (4th edn). London: Sage Publications.

Mooney, C., Briggs, M., Fletcher, M., Hansen, A. and McCullouch, J. (2012) *Primary Mathematics: Teaching Theory and Practice* (6th edn). London: Learning Matters/SAGE.

QCA (1999) *Teaching Written Calculations: Guidance for Teachers at Key Stages 1 and 2*. Sudbury: QCA Publications.

Answers

Introduction

1. Pencil-and-paper methods should develop through an inability to hold all the numbers associated with a mental calculation in your head. A child will therefore have to make jottings to support a mental calculation, but these are unlikely to bear any resemblance to the traditional written approaches. For example when mentally calculating 175 − 138 by counting on from the lower number to the higher, a child might make a note of the steps 2 (from 138 to 140), 30 (from 140 to 170) and 5 (from 170 to 175), before finally adding the steps mentally. Another example is where a child doubling 376 mentally partitions the number and doubles each part, but has to make a note of the three answers (600, 140 and 12) in order to add them together to get the final answers. These sorts of jottings should be the first stages of pencil-and-paper calculation, not the traditional methods set out in columns.

2. Appropriate models and images should be used with children of all ages to support their mathematical understanding. In the first example described for question 1 above, an empty number line could be drawn by the child to record the steps when counting on from 138 to 175. In the second example, place value cards could be used by the teacher to partition 376 into 300, 70 and 6 when modelling the procedure to children. These are just two examples of the many models and images that can be used to support the development of pencil-and-paper calculation.

3. There is little point in persevering with any method that does not yield correct answers; a broad principle that should be applied to any arithmetical process. So, for example, if a child is unable to use the traditional long multiplication method correctly, but is comfortable with the informal grid method, then it is better to pursue the latter if it continues to yield correct answers. However, in addition to precision, there are other things to consider such as efficiency and conceptual understanding. If a child is getting correct answers by using a very inefficient method (for example using pencil and paper to calculate 27 × 13 by repeatedly adding 13s), a more efficient alternative should be taught. In terms of conceptual understanding, teachers need to be aware of the fact that with some methods there is the danger of children simply following rules blindly, with little or no understanding and so when these rules are forgotten, or applied inaccurately, or when faced with a situation which requires a deviation from the rules, the child is left with nowhere to go.

4. It is tempting to think that mental methods relate only to small numbers and so bigger numbers automatically mean that pencil and paper should be used, but this is not the case. Consider calculations such as 7103 − 6998 and 4000 × 2000, which both involve relatively large numbers, but can be tackled far more speedily and efficiently using a mental method than with pencil and paper.

5. As discussed in question 1 above, pencil-and-paper calculations develop naturally from children's mental methods and so should be seen as the next stage in the progression of their arithmetical skills. Thus early pencil-and-paper approaches are essentially mental methods presented in written form, and so the skills employed will be very similar to those that have already been developed.

Section 1: informal pencil-and-paper strategies for addition and subtraction

6. An empty number line (ENL) is a powerful visual image that can be used with children to support the teaching of both addition and subtraction. In the case of 57 + 38 the procedure is likely to involve marking 57 on the number line and then counting on a further 38 to find the answer. The 38 could be partitioned into 30 and 8, thus allowing the 30 to be added first, followed by the 8, or the other way round, as illustrated in the two diagrams below.

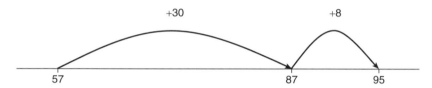

Figure 3

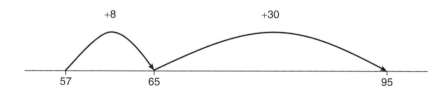

Figure 4

Another possibility is to start at 57, count on 40 and then back 2, as illustrated below.

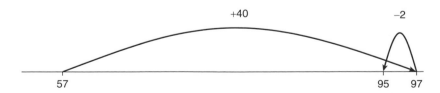

Figure 5

In these ENL diagrams it is sometimes helpful to include arrows to indicate the direction of the counting, as in the third example above.

Another issue for you to consider is how you would have tackled 38 + 57. The key point here is that addition is commutative and so it makes sense for the bigger number to be the starting point on the ENL. Children are taught this principle from an early age when told to 'hold the big number in your head'.

7. Here are the key points when modelling 85 − 37 using the ENL presented in question 7:

- Ensure the children understand subtraction as 'taking away' and so understand that the answer can be found by starting at 85 and counting back 37.

- Mark 85 on the ENL.

- Partition 37 into 30 and 7.

- Ask the children to start at 85 and count back 30, counting in 10s, and record this on the ENL.

- Ask the children to start at 55 and count back 7, counting in 1s, and record this on the ENL. This gives the final answer of 48.

A valuable visual aid to support this approach is a set of place value cards to reinforce the partitioning of 37 into 30 and 7. A 100-square could also be used when counting back in 10s from 85, by simply moving vertically down the column. Similarly the 100-square could be used when counting back in 1s from 55, by moving horizontally.

8. Here are the key points when modelling 85 − 37 using the ENL presented in question 8:

- Ensure the children understand subtraction as 'difference' and so understand that the answer can be thought of as the gap between 37 and 85.

- Mark both numbers on the ENL.

- Ask the children to identify the next multiple of 10 that comes after 37 and mark this (40) on the ENL.

- Ask the children to work out the gap between 37 and 40 and record this (3) on the ENL.

- Ask the children to identify the multiple of 10 that comes before 85 and mark this (80) on the ENL.

- Ask the children to work out the gap between 40 and 80 and record this (40) on the ENL.

- Ask the children to work out the gap between 80 and 85 and record this (5) on the ENL.

- Calculate the sum of the three gaps recorded (3 + 40 + 5) to give the final answer of 48.

A slight variation on this method would be to find the difference between 37 and 85 by counting back from 85 instead of counting forwards from 37. Children must understand that both these approaches produce the same answer.

A valuable visual aid to support both these approaches is a 100-square. This could be used to model counting on from 37 to 40 (move horizontally across the 100-square, counting in 1s), then counting on from 40 to 80 (move down vertically, counting in 10s), and finally counting on from 80 to 85 (move horizontally, counting in 1s). The 100-square can be used in a similar fashion to count back from 85 to 37.

9. Here is a possible ENL for calculating 726 − 359: the three steps can be added to give the final answer − i.e. 41 + 300 + 26 = 367.

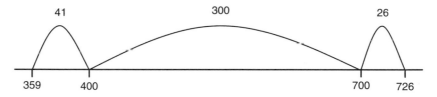

Figure 6

10. In this example the teacher has partitioned 57 into 50 and 7, and partitioned 38 into 30 and 8. The 10s and 1s have then been added separately to give 80 and 15. These are added to give the final answer 95. A valuable visual aid to support this approach is a set of place value cards to model the partitioning process. The same approach has been used here to calculate 345 + 482:

$$345 + 482 \; = \; 300 + 40 + 5 + 400 + 80 + 2$$
$$= \; 700 + 120 + 7$$
$$= \; 827$$

11. Here is an expanded vertical method for 57 + 38:

$$
\begin{array}{r}
5\,7 \\
+\ 3\,8 \\
\hline
8\,0 \\
+\ 1\,5 \\
\hline
9\,5 \\
\hline
\end{array}
$$

Say '50 plus 30 equals 80'
Say '7 plus 8 equals 15'
Mentally add 80 and 15

Here is an expanded vertical method for 345 + 482:

$$
\begin{array}{r}
345 \\
+\ 482 \\
\hline
700 \\
120 \\
+\ \ \ 7 \\
\hline
827 \\
\end{array}
$$

700	Say '300 plus 400 equals 700'
120	Say '40 plus 80 equals 120'
7	Say '5 plus 2 equals 7'

12. In both the examples in question 11 it would make no difference at all if the 1s (units) were added first. The same intermediate answers would be generated and these can be added in any order because addition is associative. The traditional compact written method for addition, usually involving carrying, requires children to always start with the 1s, but with the expanded method this is not necessary.

Also note that the expanded vertical method produces the same intermediate answers as the expanded horizontal method. Essentially they are the same method, but set out in a slightly different way.

The expanded vertical method bears a strong resemblance to the traditional compact written method. Instead of having two or three rows of intermediate answers, the traditional compact method condenses these in the form of the 'carries'. Given that the majority of difficulties that children encounter when using the traditional method are related to the carrying aspect, it is worth considering whether the expanded method provides a more accessible alternative.

13. In this example the teacher is calculating 85 − 37 by considering subtraction as 'difference' and counting on from 37 to 85. However, instead of using an ENL, as in question 8, the teacher is counting on, recording the steps, but without actually drawing the ENL. The working out in question 13 comprises the same numbers as the diagram in question 8, but rotated through 90 degrees and without the ENL itself.

14. Here is an expanded vertical method for 726 − 359:

$$
\begin{array}{ll}
359 & \\
& (+41) \\
400 & \\
& (+300) \\
700 & \\
& (+26) \\
726 & \\
\multicolumn{2}{c}{(\text{Total } 367)}
\end{array}
$$

The numbers in the working out above are the same as in the ENL in question 9, but rotated through 90 degrees.

15. Here is an explanation of the method presented in question 15:

$726 - 359 =$

$$
\begin{array}{r}
726 \\
- 359 \\
\hline
400 \\
-30 \\
-3 \\
\hline
367 \\
\end{array}
$$

400   Say '700 subtract 300 equals 400'
-30   Say '20 subtract 50 equals negative 30'
-3   Say '6 subtract 9 equals negative 3'
367   Combine 400, -30 and -3 to give 367

Here the same method has been used to calculate $1047 - 388$:

$$
\begin{array}{r}
1047 \\
- \ \ 388 \\
\hline
700 \\
-40 \\
-1 \\
\hline
659 \\
\end{array}
$$

700   '1000 subtract 300 equals 700'
-40   '40 subtract 80 equals negative 40'
-1   '7 subtract 8 equals negative 1'
659   Combine 700, -40 and -1 to give 659

Section 2: informal pencil-and-paper strategies for multiplication and division

16. The teacher has modelled the multiplication by first partitioning 76 into 70 and 6, and then multiplying each of these by 8. Finally, the two answers, 560 and 48 are added to give the answer 608. This expanded horizontal method for multiplication is based on the distributive law – that is, multiplication by 8 has been distributed over the addition of 70 and 6. A valuable visual aid to support this approach is a set of place value cards to model the partitioning process. The same approach has been used here to calculate 7×647:

$$7 \times 647 = 7 \times 600 + 7 \times 40 + 7 \times 7$$

$$= 4200 + 280 + 49$$

$$= 4529$$

17. Here is an expanded vertical method for 8×76:

$$
\begin{array}{r}
76 \\
\times \ \ 8 \\
\hline
560 \\
+ \ 48 \\
\hline
608 \\
\end{array}
$$

560   Say '8 multiplied by 70 equals 560'
48   Say '8 multiplied by 6 equals 48'

Here is an expanded vertical method for 7×647:

$$
\begin{array}{r}
647 \\
\times \quad 7 \\
\hline
4200 \\
280 \\
+ \quad 49 \\
\hline
4529 \\
\end{array}
$$

Say '7 multiplied by 600 equals 4200'
Say '7 multiplied by 40 equals 280'
Say '7 multiplied by 7 equals 49'

18. In both the examples in question 17 it would make no difference at all if the 1s (units) were added first. The same intermediate answers would be generated and these can be added in any order because addition is associative. The traditional compact written method for short multiplication, usually involving carrying, requires children to always start with the 1s, but with the expanded method this is not necessary.

You've probably spotted that the expanded vertical method produces the same intermediate answers as the expanded horizontal method. They are, in effect, the same method, but set out in a slightly different way.

As was the case for addition, discussed in questions 10 and 11, the expanded vertical method for multiplication bears a strong resemblance to the traditional compact written method. Instead of having two or three rows of intermediate answers, the traditional compact method condenses these in the form of the 'carries'. As discussed earlier, given that the majority of the difficulties that children encounter when using the traditional method are related to the carrying aspect, it is worth considering whether the expanded method provides a better alternative for some children.

19. Here the grid method of multiplication has been used to calculate 48×63:

Partition 48 into 40 and 8

Partition 63 into 60 and 3

Use these to produce a multiplication grid:

×	60	3
40		
8		

Calculate the answers for each cell:

×	60	3
40	2400	120
8	480	24

Add the 4 answers in any order, looking for numbers that can be added easily (e.g. $480 + 120 = 600$, then $2400 + 600 = 3000$) to give the final answer 3024.

20. Here the grid method of multiplication has been used to calculate 352×89:

Partition 352 into 300, 50 and 2

Partition 89 into 80 and 9

Use these to produce a multiplication grid:

×	80	9
300		
50		
2		

Calculate the answers for each cell:

×	80	9
300	24,000	2700
50	4000	450
2	160	18

Add the 6 answers in any order, looking for numbers that can be added easily (e.g. $24,000 + 4000 + 2700 = 30,700$, then $450 + 160 = 610$, then $30,700 + 610 = 31,310$, and finally add 18) to give the answer 31,328.

21. It is possible to use an expanded horizontal or vertical method when multiplying by more than a single digit, although the working out can start to look rather complex, as illustrated by the two examples below:

$$
\begin{aligned}
48 \times 63 &= (40 + 8) \times (60 + 3) \\
&= 40 \times 60 + 40 \times 3 + 8 \times 60 + 8 \times 3 \\
&= 2400 + 120 + 480 + 24 \\
&= 3024
\end{aligned}
$$

$$
\begin{aligned}
352 \times 89 &= (300 + 50 + 2) \times (80 + 9) \\
&= 300 \times 80 + 300 \times 9 + 50 \times 80 + 50 \times 9 + 2 \times 80 + 2 \times 9 \\
&= 24,000 + 2700 + 4000 + 450 + 160 + 18 \\
&= 31,328
\end{aligned}
$$

Note that the answers in the third row of each calculation are the same as the answers in the corresponding grids in questions 19 and 20. This expanded method generates the same intermediate answers as the grid method, but the way that it is set out may lead to confusion because it is more difficult to keep track of the individual multiplications. With the grid method it is less likely that any of the individual multiplications will be accidentally missed out because the grid clearly presents a cell for each one.

22. The child has first worked out 50×63 by first multiplying 63 by 100 to give 6300 and then halving the answer to give 3150. The child has then recognised that 48×63 is equivalent to $(50 \times 63) - (2 \times 63)$ and so has subtracted 126 from 3150.

The second stage of this method is based on the distributive law, more specifically the fact that multiplication by 63 can be distributed over the subtraction of 2 from 50. This is explained by the working out below:

$$
\begin{aligned}
63 \times 48 \ &= \ 63 \times (50 - 2) \\
&= \ 63 \times 50 - 63 \times 2 \\
&= \ 3150 - 126 \\
&= \ 3024
\end{aligned}
$$

A similar method could be used to calculate 352×89 by thinking of it as 100 lots of 352 and then subtracting 11 lots of 352, as illustrated below:

$$
\begin{aligned}
352 \times 89 \ &= \ 352 \times (100 - 11) \\
&= \ 352 \times 100 - 352 \times 11 \\
&= \ 35{,}200 - 3520 - 352 \ (\text{i.e. 100 lots, subtract 10 lots, subtract 1 lot}) \\
&= \ 31{,}328
\end{aligned}
$$

23. The child understands that the calculation $349 \div 56$ is asking 'how many lots of 56 are there in 349?' and so is using repeated subtraction to calculate this. In doing so, the child is thinking of division as 'grouping' as opposed to 'sharing' (see Chapter 1 for a more detailed discussion of this).

Repeated subtraction has been used here to calculate $363 \div 65$:

363	298	233	168	103
− 65	− 65	− 65	− 65	− 65
298	233	168	103	38

$363 \div 65 = 5$ remainder 38.

In technical terms there is nothing wrong with this method because, if executed correctly, it will produce correct answers. However, it is not a particularly efficient method because it could require an excessively large number of subtractions to be carried out. This in turn increases the likelihood of making a careless mistake.

24. This child is also thinking of division as grouping, but instead of repeatedly subtracting single lots of 56, she first subtracts 5 lots and then 1 lot. Presumably she has used 5 lots because she was able to calculate this quickly using mental skills, based on the fact that 10 lots of 56 is 560, so 5 lots must be half of that.

This method is often referred to as the 'chunking' method, because chunks of the divisor are subtracted, rather than single amounts.

The chunking method has been used below to calculate $1132 \div 68$:

$$
\begin{array}{rl}
1132 & \\
-\;\;\;680 & (10 \times 68) \\
\hline
452 & \\
-\;\;\;340 & (5 \times 68) \\
\hline
112 & \\
-\;\;\;\;\;68 & (1 \times 68) \\
\hline
44 & \\
\end{array}
$$

$1132 \div 68 = 16$ remainder 44.

Your own working out may be slightly different from that presented above because the size of the chunks is a matter of personal choice.

25. Here the chunking method has been used to calculate $873 \div 7$:

$$
\begin{array}{rl}
873 & \\
-\;\;700 & (100 \times 7) \\
\hline
173 & \\
-\;\;140 & (20 \times 7) \\
\hline
33 & \\
-\;\;\;28 & (4 \times 7) \\
\hline
5 & \\
\end{array}
$$

$873 \div 7 = 124$ remainder 5

Here the chunking method has been used to calculate $6562 \div 43$:

$$
\begin{array}{rl}
6562 & \\
-\;4300 & (100 \times 43) \\
\hline
2262 & \\
-\;2150 & (50 \times 43) \\
\hline
112 & \\
-\;\;\;86 & (2 \times 43) \\
\hline
26 & \\
\end{array}
$$

$6562 \div 43 = 152$ remainder 26.

4 Traditional pencil-and-paper calculation

Learning outcomes

This chapter will help you to:

- understand some of the issues associated with the use of traditional pencil-and-paper calculation;
- audit your understanding of, and ability to use, traditional pencil-and-paper calculation;
- identify strategies and resources to develop your knowledge, skills and understanding in relation to traditional pencil-and-paper calculation.

Introduction

Before auditing your knowledge and skills in relation to traditional pencil-and-paper methods, let us first consider a few general issues in relation to this aspect of calculation.

Agree/disagree

Read the following statements and decide whether you agree or disagree with each one. Then compare your thoughts with the notes provided at the end of the chapter.

1. Traditional pencil-and-paper calculation requires a thorough understanding of place value and the number system.

2. Traditional pencil-and-paper calculation helps children to develop their mental skills.

3. In order to use traditional pencil-and-paper methods you need to understand how these work.

4. The traditional pencil-and-paper methods comprise straightforward sets of rules that all children can follow easily.

5. Being able to use traditional pencil-and-paper methods is something that all children should aspire to, because these provide the best way of tackling any calculation.

Section 1: traditional pencil-and-paper methods for addition and subtraction

Answer each of the following questions and then compare your responses with those provided at the end of the chapter.

6. Calculate $487 + 639$ using the traditional pencil-and-paper method, with one number underneath the other and possibly involving 'carrying'. Do you know of any slight variations in the way that the calculation can be set out?

7. First read the solution and explanatory notes provided at the end of the chapter relating to question 6, so that you are aware of the traditional method for addition. Then try these additions using the same approach:

   (a) $324 + 149$ (b) $3052 + 865$ (c) $6907 + 458 + 1839$

8. All the children in a class calculated $547 + 286$. Here are the solutions provided by three children. Can you see where each child has gone wrong?

   Child A

   $$\begin{array}{r} 5\ 4\ 7 \\ +\ 2_1\,8_1\,6 \\ \hline 7\ 2\ 3 \end{array}$$

   Child B

   $$\begin{array}{r} 5\ 4\ 7 \\ +\quad 2\ 8\ 6 \\ \hline 7\ 1\ 2\ 1\ 3 \end{array}$$

   Child C

   $$\begin{array}{r} 5\ 4\ 7 \\ +\quad 2_5\,8_3\,6 \\ \hline 1\ 2\ 1\ 1 \end{array}$$

9. Calculate $753 - 436$ using the traditional pencil-and-paper method, with one number underneath the other and possibly involving 'borrowing' (or 'exchanging'). Do you know the correct name for this method and how the procedure actually works? What happens to the top number when you 'borrow' or 'exchange'?

10. First read the solution and explanatory notes provided at the end of the chapter relating to question 9, so that you are aware of the traditional method for subtraction by decomposition. Then try these subtractions using the same approach:

   (a) $372 - 158$ (b) $6315 - 2538$ (c) $8602 - 2347$

11. All the children in a class calculated $703 - 487$. Here are the solutions provided by three children. Can you see where each child has gone wrong?

Child A

$$
\begin{array}{r}
7\,0\,3 \\
-4\,8\,7 \\
\hline
3\,8\,4 \\
\hline
\end{array}
$$

Child B

$$
\begin{array}{r}
{}^5\!\!\not{7}\ {}^1 0\ {}^1 3 \\
-\ 4\ \ 8\ \ 7 \\
\hline
1\ \ 2\ \ 6 \\
\hline
\end{array}
$$

Child C

$$
\begin{array}{r}
{}^6\!\!\not{7}\ 0\ {}^1 3 \\
-\ 4\ \ 8\ \ 7 \\
\hline
2\ \ 8\ \ 6 \\
\hline
\end{array}
$$

12. A teacher asked the children in her class to complete some subtractions for their homework, using the traditional pencil-and-paper method. The next day one child presented the following working out for $536 - 279$ and said that her mum had shown her to do it this way.

$$
\begin{array}{r}
5\ {}^1 3\ {}^1 6 \\
-\ {}_1 2\ {}_1 7\ 9 \\
\hline
2\ \ 5\ \ 7 \\
\hline
\end{array}
$$

Are you familiar with this written method? Even if you are not familiar with it, can you work out the procedure?

Section 2: traditional pencil-and-paper methods for multiplication and division

Answer each of the following questions and then compare your responses with those provided at the end of the chapter.

13. Calculate 573×8 using the traditional pencil-and-paper method for short multiplication, with one number underneath the other and involving 'carrying'. Do you know of any slight variations in the way that the calculation can be set out?

14. First read the solution and explanatory notes provided at the end of the chapter relating to question 13, so that you are aware of the traditional

method for short multiplication. Then try these multiplications using the same approach:

(a) 409×6 (b) 3724×7 (c) 843×12

15. Calculate 715×34 using the traditional pencil-and-paper method for long multiplication, with one number underneath the other and involving 'carrying'.

16. First read the solution and explanatory notes provided at the end of the chapter relating to question 15, so that you are aware of the traditional method for long multiplication. Then try these multiplications using the same approach:

(a) 436×27 (b) 2169×45 (c) 3614×108

17. Calculate $772 \div 9$ using the traditional pencil-and-paper method for short division. Do you know of any slight variations in the way the calculation can be set out?

18. First read the solution and explanatory notes provided at the end of the chapter relating to question 17, so that you are aware of the traditional method for short division. Then try these divisions using the same approach:

(a) $988 \div 7$ (b) $5803 \div 4$ (c) $6450 \div 12$

19. Calculate $985 \div 23$ using the traditional pencil-and-paper method for long division.

20. First read the solution and explanatory notes provided at the end of the chapter relating to question 19, so that you are aware of the traditional method for long division. Then try these divisions using the same approach:

(a) $1397 \div 41$ (b) $5061 \div 38$ (c) $2847 \div 26$

What to do next?
Developing your own subject knowledge

If, having tackled the questions in this chapter, you feel that you still need to develop your ability to understand and use traditional pencil-and-paper techniques, it is recommended that you read *Teaching Arithmetic in Primary Schools*, Chapter 5 ('Traditional pencil-and-paper arithmetic'). In particular this chapter provides:

- detailed step-by-step examples to illustrate all the traditional pencil-and-paper procedures;

- a discussion of the benefits and potential difficulties associated with traditional pencil-and-paper approaches, including a consideration of the errors that children typically make;

- research summaries and case studies which highlight some of the issues associated with the teaching of traditional pencil-and-paper approaches.

  Other sources which can contribute to the development of your own knowledge and skills include:

- *Primary Mathematics: Knowledge and Understanding*, Chapter 2 ('Number'), particularly the section called 'The four rules of number'.

- *Mathematics Explained for Primary Teachers*, Chapter 9 ('Written methods for addition and subtraction') and Chapter 12 ('Written methods for multiplication and division').

- *Understanding and Teaching Primary Mathematics,* Chapter 6 ('Calculating').

If you understand the various methods presented in this chapter but just need more practice then you can easily facilitate this yourself by generating random questions to answer. For example you could choose any pair of 3 or 4-digit numbers and add or subtract these using the traditional pencil-and-paper methods. Similarly, you could randomly pick a 3 or 4-digit number and then multiply or divide it by a 1 or 2-digit number, again using the traditional methods.

Developing your knowledge of the curriculum

Read the National Curriculum programmes of study for mathematics and try to identify those aspects that relate to traditional pencil-and-paper calculation. This starts to be mentioned explicitly in the Year 3 programme of study.

Also examine the mathematics schemes of work devised by the schools in which you work. These are likely to provide more detail than the broad outline in the National Curriculum. Read your school's mathematics documentation to see when and how the traditional pencil-and-paper methods are introduced and the stages that children are expected to pass through. Speak to the person responsible for mathematics in your school and ask about the teaching of traditional pencil-and-paper techniques. Also speak to other members of staff about the traditional methods, in particular the sorts of difficulties that children typically encounter when using them. Make arrangements to observe the teaching of traditional pencil-and-paper methods throughout Key Stage 2 and try to become involved in supporting the children, again focusing on the errors they make.

Recommended reading

Cotton, T. (2010) *Understanding and Teaching Primary Mathematics*. Harlow: Pearson Education.

English, R. (2013) *Teaching Arithmetic in Primary Schools*. London: Learning Matters/ SAGE.

Haylock, D. (2010) *Mathematics Explained for Primary Teachers* (4th edn). London: Sage Publications.

Mooney, C., Ferrie, L., Fox, S., Hansen, A. and Wrathmell, R. (2012) *Primary Mathematics: Knowledge and Understanding* (6th edn). London: Learning Matters/ SAGE.

Plunkett, S. (1979) 'Decomposition and all that rot', *Mathematics in School*, 8(3): 2–5.

QCA (1999) *Teaching Written Calculations: Guidance for Teachers at Key Stages 1 and 2*. Sudbury: QCA Publications.

Answers

Introduction

1. When following a traditional pencil-and-paper procedure, children focus on the individual digits rather than each number in its entirety. So, for example, when using the traditional method to add 583 and 346, children add the digits 3 and 6, followed by 8 and 4, and so on. In doing so, a child can obtain the correct answer, but without any appreciation of what the 5 and 8 in 583 actually represent. This means that children can follow the traditional routines to generate correct answers without any understanding of place value, or any appreciation of size and quantity in relation to the numbers they are working with.

2. Traditional pencil-and-paper calculation requires children to work only with single digits, hence the long-established requirement for young children to learn simple number bonds and multiplication facts. These are the only mental skills required to execute the traditional pencil-and-paper methods. The traditional approaches therefore play no part at all in developing the sorts of efficient mental strategies discussed in Chapter 2. Indeed it is often the case that the traditional methods have a negative effect on the development of mental skills because children abandon the latter in favour of the former, resulting in traditional methods being used for simple calculations that ought to be tackled mentally.

3. You can follow the procedures required for traditional pencil-and-paper calculation, resulting in the production of consistently correct answers, but without any understanding of how the procedures work. For example, do you know what is actually happening to the numbers when you are 'carrying' and 'borrowing' as part of the traditional written methods for addition and subtraction? Probably not, and that is almost certainly the case for the majority of children. It would be reasonable to argue that it is not necessary to know these things, in the same way that it is not necessary for a motorist to know how the internal combustion engine works. However, we need to be wary of building competence in calculation that is based solely on sets of rules and procedures which can be easily forgotten or misapplied, leaving children with nothing to fall back on.

4. Yes, the traditional pencil-and-paper methods do comprise sets of rules and procedures, but they are not always easy or straightforward for children to learn. There are numerous potential pitfalls when using these methods and so some children, despite many years of practice, are unable to follow the rules correctly and consistently. One particular example of this is subtraction when the larger number (the one on the top) has several zeros, as in 3006 − 2749. As soon as the child has to 'borrow', but finds that there is nothing to borrow from, this causes difficulties, because the specific rules relating to this particular scenario cannot be remembered. Instead of providing repeated practice of a method that the child may never fully master, why not consider an alternative approach? For example, in the case of 3006 − 2749 the answer could be calculated by counting on from the lower number to the higher, possibly using mental skills.

5. Teachers must be careful that they do not, either deliberately or unknowingly, present the traditional pencil-and-paper methods as being the 'best', the 'correct' or the 'proper' way of tackling a calculation. This can lead to children always reverting to the traditional methods, even when dealing with simple calculations or ones that can be tackled far more efficiently using an alternative approach. Consider the examples 6003 − 5976 and 498 × 3. The numbers are relatively large and so many children are likely to employ the traditional written methods to answer them. However, they can be both tackled far more quickly and efficiently using mental methods, thus avoiding the potential pitfalls associated with 'carrying' and 'borrowing' that were discussed in the response to question 4 above. When faced with any calculation children should be encouraged to ask themselves the question 'Can I do it mentally?' Possessing high-quality mental skills will serve children well in their everyday lives and is something they should aspire to.

Section 1: traditional pencil-and-paper methods for addition and subtraction

6. Here is one possible way of setting out the calculation 487 + 639, together with some explanatory notes:

4 8 7	7 add 9 equals 16. Write down 6 and carry 1.
+ 6₁ 3₁ 9	8 add 3 add 1 (carried) equals 12. Write down 2 and carry 1.
1 1 2 6	4 add 6 add 1 (carried) equals 11. Write down 11.

Slight variations on the way that this is set out relate to the carries. Some people prefer to include these at the top of each column (i.e. above the 4 and the 8 in this example) or underneath the bottom horizontal line.

7. Here are the solutions together with some explanatory notes:

(a) 324 + 149

```
  3 2 4      4 add 9 equals 13. Write down 3 and carry 1.
+ 1 4₁9      2 add 4 add 1 (carried) equals 7. Write down 7.
  4 7 3      3 add 1 equals 4. Write down 4.
```

(b) 3052 + 865

```
  3 0 5 2    2 add 5 equals 7. Write down 7.
+   8₁6 5    5 add 6 equals 11. Write down 1 and carry 1.
  3 9 1 7    0 add 8 add 1 (carried) equals 9. Write down 9.
             3 add 0 equals 3. Write down 3.
```

(c) 6907 + 458 +1839

```
  6 9 0 7    7 add 8 add 9 equals 24. Write down 4 and carry 2.
    4 5 8    0 add 5 add 3 add 2 (carried) equals 10. Write down 0 and carry 1.
+ 1₂8₁3₂9    9 add 4 add 8 add 1 (carried) equals 22. Write down 2 and carry 2.
  9 2 0 4    6 add 0 add 1 add 2 (carried) equals 9. Write down 9.
```

8. Child A has included the carries but has not remembered to include these when adding the next column of digits. Child B has avoided the carrying process altogether and just written down 2-digit answers when adding the first and second columns of numbers. Child C has used carries but has transposed the position of the two digits. For example, after adding 7 and 6 to give 13, the 1 has been written down and the 3 carried, when in fact it should be the other way round.

9. Here is the traditional pencil-and-paper method for subtraction using 'borrowing' or 'exchanging', together with some explanatory notes:

```
  7 ⁴5̶ ¹3    Subtract 6 from 3, but you can't do it, so borrow from the 5.
- 4 3 6      Cross out the 5 in the tens column to leave 4 tens. The 3 ones now
  3 1 7      becomes 13.
             Subtract 6 from 13 to leave 7. Subtract 3 from 4 to leave 1.
             Subtract 4 from 7 to leave 3.
```

The correct name for this method is subtraction by decomposition, because when you 'borrow' you decompose the top number so that it is written differently, but in numerical terms it is still the same. Initially the number 753 is written as

7 hundreds (700) 5 tens (50) 3 ones (3) which is 753.

After 'borrowing', it is now written as

7 hundreds (700) 4 tens (40) 13 ones (13) which is still 753.

The expression 'borrowing' is widely used when modelling this method, but it is not an accurate description of the process because borrowing implies that something is paid back later, which is not the case here. The term 'exchanging' is therefore a better alternative. So when modelling this particular example to children you ought to say 'Exchange one of the 5 tens for 10 ones, to give 13 in the ones column'.

10. Here are the solutions together with some explanatory notes:

(a) $372 - 158$

$3\ ^6\!7\ ^1\!2$ Subtract 8 from 2, but you can't do it, so exchange one of the 7 tens.
$-1\ \ 5\ \ 8$ Cross out the 7 in the tens column to leave 6 tens. The 2 ones now becomes 12.
$\ \ \ \ 2\ \ 1\ \ 4$ Subtract 8 from 12 to leave 4. Subtract 5 from 6 to leave 1.
           Subtract 1 from 3 to leave 2.

(b) $6315 - 2538$

$$^5\!\cancel{6}\ ^{12}\cancel{3}\ ^{10}\cancel{1}\ ^1\!5$$
$$-\ 2\ \ \ 5\ \ \ 3\ \ \ 8$$
$$\ \ \ \ 3\ \ \ 7\ \ \ 7\ \ \ 7$$

Stage 1 (the ones): subtract 8 from 5, but you can't do it, so exchange the 1 in the tens column. Cross out the 1 to leave 0 tens. The 5 ones becomes 15. Subtract 8 from 15 to leave 7.

Stage 2 (the tens): subtract 3 from 0, but you can't do it, so exchange 1 of the 3 hundreds. Cross out the 3 in the hundreds column to leave 2. The 0 tens becomes 10. Subtract 3 from 10 to leave 7.

Stage 3 (the hundreds): subtract 5 from 2, but you can't do it, so exchange 1 of the 6 thousands. Cross out the 6 in the thousands column to leave 5. The 2 hundreds becomes 12. Subtract 5 from 12 to leave 7.

Stage 4 (the thousands): subtract 2 from 5 to leave 3.

(c) $8602 - 2347$

$$8\ ^5\!\cancel{6}\ ^9\!\cancel{\cancel{1}}\cancel{0}\ ^1\!2$$
$$-2\ \ \ 3\ \ \ 4\ \ \ 7$$
$$\ \ \ 6\ \ \ 2\ \ \ 5\ \ \ 5$$

Stage 1 (the ones): subtract 7 from 2, but you can't do it, so exchange in the tens column. There are no tens, so exchange 1 of the 6 hundreds. Cross out the 6 to leave 5 hundreds. The 0 tens becomes 10. Now exchange 1 of the 10 tens. Cross out the 10 in the tens column to leave 9. The 2 ones becomes 12. Subtract 7 from 12 to leave 5.

Stage 2 (the tens): subtract 4 from 9 to leave 5.

Stage 3 (the hundreds): subtract 3 from 5 to leave 2.

Stage 4 (the thousands): subtract 2 from 8 to leave 6.

11. Child A has avoiding exchanging by always subtracting the smaller number from the larger – i.e. $7 - 3 = 4$, $8 - 0 = 8$ and $7 - 4 = 3$.

    Child B has recognised that 7 cannot be subtracted from 3 and so has exchanged 2 of the hundreds and given 1 of these to the tens and 1 to the ones. So the 7 has been crossed out in the hundreds column and replaced with 5, and then 1 has been written in the tens column and 1 in the ones column. This has completely changed the top number. It started as 703 but has been changed to 613 (5 hundreds, 10 tens, 13 ones).

    Child C has started correctly, recognising that 7 cannot be subtracted from 3, but has exchanged 1 of the hundreds for 10 ones, completely overlooking what should be done in the tens column. So, as was the case with Child B, the top number has been changed, again to 613 but in a slightly different way (6 hundreds and 13 ones). Child C has also made another mistake in the tens column, by subtracting 0 from 8 instead of 8 from 0.

12. The child's mother has used a method called 'subtraction by equal addition' which involves a process sometimes referred to as 'borrowing and paying back on the doorstep'. Here is a brief summary of the procedure when calculating $536 - 279$:

    Stage 1 (the ones): subtract 9 from 6, but you can't do it, so change the 6 to 16 by placing a 1 in front of the 6. Also place an extra ten in the tens column by writing a 1 next to the 7. Now subtract 9 from 16 to leave 7.

    Stage 2 (the tens): subtract 8 from 3 (remember, the 1 next to the 7 means it's 8 altogether). You can't do it, so change the 3 to 13 by placing a 1 in front of the 3. Also place an extra hundred in the hundreds column by writing a 1 next to the 2. Now subtract 8 from 13 to leave 5.

    Stage 3 (the hundreds): subtract 3 from 5 (remember, the 1 next to the 2 means it's 3 altogether) to leave 2.

    Can you see how this procedure works? At the first stage 10 was added to the top number by increasing the 6 to 16, but 10 was also added to the bottom number by increasing the 7 tens (70) to 8 tens (80). Similarly at the second stage each number was increased by 100. When the two numbers are increased by the same amount the difference between them remains the same, hence the name 'subtraction by equal addition'.

    This traditional method is not as popular as subtraction by decomposition, but you may come across teachers and parents who are familiar with it and so you need to be prepared for any discussions that may arise.

Section 2: traditional pencil-and-paper methods for multiplication and division

13. Here is one possible way of setting out the calculation 573 × 8, together with some explanatory notes:

        5 7 3   3 multiplied by 8 equals 24. Write down 4 and carry 2.
    ×   ₅ ₂ 8   7 multiplied by 8 equals 56, plus 2 (carried) equals 58. Write
        4 5 8 4   down 8 and carry 5.
                       5 multiplied by 8 equals 40, plus 5 (carried) equals 45. Write
                       down 45.

    Slight variations on the way that this is set out relate to the carries. Some people prefer to include these at the top of each column (i.e. above the 7 and the 5 in this example) or underneath the bottom horizontal line.

14. Here are the solutions together with some explanatory notes:

    (a) 409 × 6

        4 0 9   9 multiplied by 6 equals 54. Write down 4 and carry 5.
    ×   ₅ 6   0 multiplied by 6 equals 0, plus 5 (carried) equals 5. Write down 5.
        2 4 5 4   4 multiplied by 6 equals 24. Write down 24.

    (b) 3724 × 7

        3 7 2 4   4 multiplied by 7 equals 28. Write down 8 and carry 2.
    ×   ₅ ₁ ₂ 7   2 multiplied by 7 equals 14, plus 2 (carried) equals 16. Write down
        2 6 0 6 8   6 and carry 1.
                       7 multiplied by 7 equals 49, plus 1 (carried) equals 50. Write down
                       0 and carry 5.
                       3 multiplied by 7 equals 21, plus 5 (carried) equals 26. Write down 26.

    (c) 843 × 12

        8 4 3   3 multiplied by 12 equals 36. Write down 6 and carry 3.
    ×   ₅₃1 2   4 multiplied by 12 equals 48, plus 3 (carried) equals 51. Write
        1 0 1 1 6   down 1 and carry 5.
                       8 multiplied by 12 equals 96, plus 5 (carried) equals 101. Write
                       down 101.

    In the third example it is assumed that you know your multiplication facts up to 12 × 12, which is an expectation of children in the latest version of the National Curriculum.

15. Here is the long multiplication method for calculating 715×34, together with some explanatory notes:

```
        7 1 5
  ×     ₁ 3₂4
      2 8 6 0
    2 1₁4₁5 0
    2 4 3 1 0
```

5 multiplied by 4 equals 20. Write down 0 and carry 2.

1 multiplied by 4 equals 4, plus 2 (carried) equals 6. Write down 6.

7 multiplied by 4 equals 28. Write down 28.

Multiply by the 30 in 34, by writing down 0 and then multiplying by 3.

5 multiplied by 3 equals 15. Write down 5 and carry 1.

1 multiplied by 3 equals 3, plus 1 (carried) equals 4. Write down 4.

7 multiplied by 3 equals 21. Write down 21.

Finally, add 2860 and 21450 using the traditional method for addition.

16. Here are the solutions together with some explanatory notes:

(a) 436×27:

```
        4 3 6
  ×   ₁ ₂2₄7
      3 0 5 2
      8 7 2 0
    1 1 7 7 2
```

6 multiplied by 7 equals 42. Write down 2 and carry 4.

3 multiplied by 7 equals 21, plus 4 (carried) equals 25. Write down 5 and carry 2.

4 multiplied by 7 equals 28, plus 2 (carried) equals 30. Write down 30.

Multiply by the 20 in 27, by writing down 0 and then multiplying by 2.

6 multiplied by 2 equals 12. Write down 2 and carry 1.

3 multiplied by 2 equals 6, plus 1 (carried) equals 7. Write down 7.

4 multiplied by 2 equals 8. Write down 8.

Finally, add 3052 and 8720 using the traditional method for addition.

(b) 2169×45:

```
      2 1 6 9
  ×   ₂₃₃₄4 5
    1 0 8 4 5
    8 6₁7₁6 0
    9 7 6 0 5
```

9 multiplied by 5 equals 45. Write down 5 and carry 4.

6 multiplied by 5 equals 30, plus 4 (carried) equals 34. Write down 4 and carry 3.

1 multiplied by 5 equals 5, plus 3 (carried) equals 8. Write down 8.

2 multiplied by 5 equals 10. Write down 10.

Multiply by the 40 in 45, by writing down 0 and then multiplying by 4.

9 multiplied by 4 equals 36. Write down 6 and carry 3.

6 multiplied by 4 equals 24, plus 3 (carried) equals 27. Write down 7 and carry 2.

1 multiplied by 4 equals 4, plus 2 (carried) equals 6. Write down 6.

2 multiplied by 4 equals 8. Write down 8.

Finally, add 10845 and 86760 using the traditional method for addition.

(c) 3614 × 108:

```
        3 6 1 4
  ×     4 1₁0₃8
      2 8 9 1 2
    3 6₁1₁4 0 0
    3 9 0 3 1 2
```

4 multiplied by 8 equals 32. Write down 2 and carry 3.

1 multiplied by 8 equals 8, plus 3 (carried) equals 11. Write down 1 and carry 1.

6 multiplied by 8 equals 48, plus 1 (carried) equals 49. Write down 9 and carry 4.

3 multiplied by 8 equals 24, plus 4 (carried) equals 28. Write down 28.

It is not necessary to multiply by the 0 in 108 because the answer will be 0.

Multiply by the 100 in 108, by writing down two 0s and then multiplying by 1.

3614 multiplied by 1 equals 3614.

Do this as a single calculation rather than 4 separate ones, and write down 3614.

Finally, add 28912 and 361400 using the traditional method for addition.

17. Here is the short division method for calculating 772 ÷ 9, together with some explanatory notes:

```
      8  5  r 7
  9)7 7⁵ 2
```

77 divided by 9 is 8 remainder 5.

Write 8 above the line and squeeze the remainder 5 in front of the 2.

52 divided by 9 is 5 remainder 7.

Write 5 above the line and record the remainder 7.

An alternative way of setting out the same short division calculation is presented below:

```
9 )7 7⁵ 2
    8  5  r 7
```

18. Here are the solutions together with some explanatory notes:

(a) 988 ÷ 7

```
     1  4  1 r  1
  7)9²8 8
```

9 divided by 7 is 1 remainder 2.

Write 1 above the line and squeeze the remainder 2 in front of the 8.

28 divided by 7 is 4 with no remainder. Write 4 above the line.

8 divided by 7 is 1 remainder 1.

Write 1 above the line and record the remainder 1.

(b) 5803 ÷ 4

$$\frac{1\ 4\ 5\ 0\ r\ 3}{4\overline{)5^18^20\ 3}}$$

5 divided by 4 is 1 remainder 1.

Write 1 above the line and squeeze the remainder 1 in front of the 8.

18 divided by 4 is 4 remainder 2.

Write 4 above the line and squeeze the remainder 2 in front of the 0.

20 divided by 4 is 5, with no remainder. Write 5 above the line.

3 divided by 4 is 0 remainder 3.

Write 0 above the line and record the remainder 3.

(c) 6450 ÷ 12

$$\frac{5\ 3\ 7\ r\ 6}{12\overline{)6\ 4^45^90}}$$

64 divided by 12 is 5 remainder 4.

Write 5 above the line and squeeze the remainder 4 in front of the 5.

45 divided by 12 is 3 remainder 9.

Write 3 above the line and squeeze the remainder 9 in front of the 0.

90 divided by 12 is 7 remainder 6.

Write 7 above the line and record the remainder 6.

In the third example it is assumed that you know your division facts corresponding to the multiplication facts up to 12 × 12, which is an expectation of children in the latest version of the National Curriculum.

19. Here is the long division method for calculating 985 ÷ 23, together with some explanatory notes:

$$\begin{array}{r} 42 \\ 23\overline{)985} \\ -92\!\downarrow \\ \hline 65 \\ -46 \\ \hline 19 \end{array}$$

98 divided by 23 is 4.

23 multiplied by 4 is 92. Write 92 below the 98.

Subtract 92 from 98 to give the remainder 6.

Instead of squeezing the remainder (6) in front of the 5, drop the 5 down so that it appears after the 6, and it becomes 65.

65 divided by 23 equals 2.

23 multiplied by 2 is 46. Write 46 below the 65.

Subtract 46 from 65 to give the remainder 8.

The answer is 42 r 19.

20. Here are the solutions together with some explanatory notes:

(a) 1397 ÷ 41

```
        3 4
41)1 3 9 7
   − 1 2 3 ↓
      1 6 7
   − 1 6 4
          3
```

139 divided by 41 is 3.

41 multiplied by 3 is 123. Write 123 below the 139.

Subtract 123 from 139 to give the remainder 16.

Instead of squeezing the remainder (16) in front of the 7, drop the 7 down so that it appears after the 16, and it becomes 167.

167 divided by 41 equals 4.

41 multiplied by 4 is 164. Write 164 below the 167.

Subtract 164 from 167 to give the remainder 3.

The answer is 34 r 3.

(b) 5061 ÷ 38

```
        1 3 3
38)5 0 6 1
   − 3 8 ↓ ↓
      1 2 6
   − 1 1 4
      1 2 1
   − 1 1 4
          7
```

50 divided by 38 is 1.

38 multiplied by 1 is 38. Write 38 below the 50.

Subtract 38 from 50 to give the remainder 12.

Instead of squeezing the remainder (12) in front of the 6, drop the 6 down so that it appears after the 12, and it becomes 126.

126 divided by 38 equals 3.

38 multiplied by 3 is 114. Write 114 below the 126.

Subtract 114 from 126 to give the remainder 12.

Drop the 1 down so it appears after the 12, and it becomes 121.

121 divided by 38 equals 3.

38 multiplied by 3 is 114. Write 114 below the 121.

Subtract 114 from 121 to give the remainder 7.

The answer is 133 r 7.

(c) 2847 ÷ 26

```
        1 0 9
26)2 8 4 7
   − 2 6 ↓ ↓
      2 4 7
   − 2 3 4
        1 3
```

28 divided by 26 is 1.

26 multiplied by 1 is 26. Write 26 below the 28.

Subtract 26 from 28 to give the remainder 2.

Instead of squeezing the remainder (2) in front of the 4, drop the 4 down so that it appears after the 2, and it becomes 24.

24 divided by 26 equals 0, with a remainder of 24.

Drop the 7 down so it appears after the 24, and it becomes 247.

247 divided by 26 equals 9.

26 multiplied by 9 is 234. Write 234 below the 247.

Subtract 234 from 247 to give the remainder 13.

The answer is 109 r 13.

5 Calculating with fractions, decimals, percentages and ratios

Learning outcomes

This chapter will help you to:

- understand some of the general issues associated with the teaching of calculation involving fractions, decimals, percentages and ratios;
- audit your ability to carry out calculations involving fractions, decimals, percentages and ratios;
- identify strategies and resources to develop your knowledge, skills and understanding in relation to calculating with fractions, decimals, percentages and ratios.

Introduction

Before auditing your knowledge and skills in relation to fractions, decimals, percentages and ratios, let us first consider a few general issues in relation to this aspect of calculation.

Agree/disagree

Read the following statements and decide whether you agree or disagree with each one. Then compare your thoughts with the notes provided at the end of the chapter.

1. Place value is a concept that only applies to whole numbers and so this work should be restricted to KS1 and lower KS2.

2. Calculations involving fractions are challenging and so children should not be introduced to fractions until upper KS2.

3. Instant recall of number facts and mental calculation is not relevant to fractions, decimals and percentages because pencil-and-paper methods should always be the recommended approach.

4. Ratio and proportion are different words to describe the same mathematical concept.

5. Fractions and percentages are completely different concepts and so require different teaching approaches.

6. Models and images are not necessary when teaching fractions, decimals, percentages and ratios because the calculations can be carried out easily without them.

Section 1: calculating with fractions

Answer each of the following questions and then compare your responses with those provided at the end of the chapter.

7. (a) What fraction of this grid is shaded?

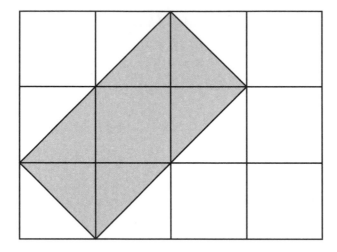

Figure 1

(b) There are 35 children in a class. 25 of them stop at school for lunch. What fraction of the children stop for lunch?

(c) A class comprises 12 boys and 20 girls. What fraction of the class is boys?

8. Arrange these fractions in order of size, starting with the smallest:

$$\frac{3}{4} \qquad \frac{2}{3} \qquad \frac{7}{12} \qquad \frac{5}{8}$$

9. One-third of the children in a school have hot dinners. One-quarter bring a packed lunch. The rest go home for lunch. What fraction of the children go home?

10. (a) What is one-fifth of 900 kg?

(b) What is three-quarters of £75?

(c) What is five-eighths of 144 km?

11. Calculate the answers to each of the following:

(a) $\frac{5}{6} - \frac{1}{3}$ (b) $1\frac{3}{8} + 3\frac{1}{2}$ (c) $1\frac{3}{4} + 2\frac{2}{3}$

12. Calculate the answers to each of the following:

(a) $3 \times \frac{3}{4}$ (b) $1\frac{5}{8} \times 2$ (c) $\frac{3}{4} \times \frac{2}{5}$

13. Calculate the answers to each of the following.

(a) $\frac{3}{4} \div 2$ (b) $2\frac{2}{5} \div 3$ (c) $1\frac{2}{3} \div 4$

Section 2: calculating with decimals

Answer each of the following questions and then compare your responses with those provided at the end of the chapter.

14. Here are some numbers:

    0.01   0.09   0.11   0.99   0.1   0.001

    (a) Arrange them in order of size, starting with the smallest.

    (b) Which two numbers are closest to one another?

    (c) Which two numbers have a sum of 1?

15. Calculate the answers to these questions using mental methods. The only thing you should write down is the answer:

    (a) $4.65 + 1.2 + 0.35$;

    (b) $10.1 - 9.85$;

    (c) 7.89×3;

    (d) $2.75 \div 0.25$.

16. Calculate the answers to these questions. Feel free to use any pencil-and-paper methods you wish:

    (a) $13.8 + 5.326$;

    (b) $9.4 - 6.18$;

    (c) 58.6×2.4;

    (d) $24.36 \div 7$.

Section 3: calculating with percentages

Answer each of the following questions and then compare your responses with those provided at the end of the chapter.

17. (a) What percentage of this grid is shaded?

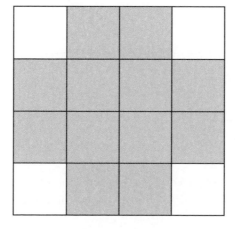

Figure 2

(b) A child scores 17 out of 20 in a test. What is the child's percentage score?

(c) In KS1 75 children stop at school for lunch and 45 go home. What percentage of children stop at school?

18. (a) What is 75% of £250?

(b) What is 35% of £120?

(c) What is 17½% of £48?

19. (a) Somebody earns £380 and receives a 5% pay rise. What is the new weekly wage?

(b) A coat costs £85 but is reduced by 20% in the sale. What is the sale price?

(c) The cost of a meal is £56 plus a 15% service charge. What is the final cost of the meal?

20. A bicycle is reduced in the sale by 25%. The sale price is £270. What was the original price?

21. A mobile phone costs £174, including 20% VAT. What was the price before the VAT was added?

Section 4: calculating with ratios

Answer each of the following questions and then compare your responses with those provided at the end of the chapter.

22. (a) A class comprises 12 boys and 20 girls. What is the ratio of boys to girls?

(b) In the grid below, what is the ratio of grey to white?

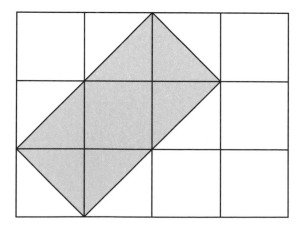

Figure 3

(c) There are 35 children in a class. 25 of them stop at school for lunch and the rest go home. What is the ratio of children who stop for lunch to children who go home?

23. To make jam you need to use strawberries and sugar in the ratio 3:4.

    (a) If you have got 12 kg of strawberries, how much sugar do you need?

    (b) Someone makes jam using 9 kg more sugar than strawberries. How much of each ingredient is used?

    (c) If you have got 15 kg of sugar, what weight of strawberries do you need?

24. The scale on a map is 1:500,000.

    (a) The distance between two villages on the map is 2.5 cm. What is the actual distance between the two villages?

    (b) The real distance between two towns is 28 km. How far apart are they on the map?

25. A recipe to make biscuits requires flour, sugar and butter in the ratio 4:1:3. The complete mixture weighs 1 kg. What is the weight of each ingredient?

What to do next?

Developing your own subject knowledge

If, after tackling the questions in this chapter, you still feel that you need to develop your knowledge and understanding of fractions, decimals, percentages and ratios, it is recommended that you read *Teaching Arithmetic in Primary Schools*, Chapter 6 ('Arithmetic with fractions, decimals, percentages and ratios'). This chapter provides:

- a discussion of the essential prerequisite knowledge and understanding that children must possess in relation to fractions, decimals, percentages and ratios before they are introduced to calculation;

- detailed step-by-step examples to illustrate a range of procedures for calculating with fractions, decimals, percentages and ratios;

- research summaries and case studies which highlight some of the issues associated with the teaching and learning of fractions, decimals, percentages and ratios.

Other sources which can contribute to the development of your own knowledge and skills in this area include:

- *The Primary Teacher's Guide to Number*, Chapter 3 ('Fractions, decimals, percentages and ratios') which includes valuable sections on language, notation, key concepts and calculations.

- *Primary Mathematics: Knowledge and Understanding*, Chapter 2 ('Number'), particularly the sections called 'Fractions', 'Decimals', 'Percentages' and 'Ratio and proportion'.

- *Mathematics Explained for Primary Teachers*, Chapter 17 ('Fractions and ratios'), Chapter 18 ('Calculations with decimals') and Chapter 19 ('Proportions and percentages').

- *Teaching Children to Calculate Mentally*, Chapter 4 ('Multiplication and division strategies'), particularly the section called 'Fractions, decimals and percentages'.

- *Teaching Mental Calculation Strategies: Guidance for Teachers at Key Stages 1 and 2*, Part 4 ('Teaching multiplication and division skills and strategies'), particularly the section called 'Fractions, decimals and percentages'.

- *Teaching Written Calculations: Guidance for Teachers at Key Stages 1 and 2*, Part 5 ('Fractions, decimals and percentages').

Developing your knowledge of the curriculum

Read the National Curriculum programmes of study for mathematics and try to identify those aspects that relate to fractions, decimals, percentages and ratios. You will have to read the sections for every year group because the earliest mention of fractions is in the year 1 programme of study. Identify the progression in children's knowledge, skills and understanding from year 1 through to year 6 and also ensure that you possess the necessary subject knowledge to teach these aspects of mathematics.

The programmes of study provide only a broad outline of what should be taught and so you should find more detail in your school's own schemes of work for mathematics. Again, identify the stages that children are expected to pass through in relation to fractions, decimals, percentages and ratios. Also speak to staff in your placement schools about these aspects of mathematics. What are the typical errors and misconceptions that children demonstrate? Do experienced teachers find these topics challenging to master and if so, how do they go about developing their own expertise and confidence to equip them to teach effectively?

Recommended reading

DfE (2010) *Teaching Children to Calculate Mentally*. London: DfE Publications.

English, R. (2012) *The Primary Teacher's Guide to Number*. Whitney: Scholastic.

English, R. (2013) *Teaching Arithmetic in Primary Schools*. London: Learning Matters/ SAGE.

Haylock, D. (2010) *Mathematics Explained for Primary Teachers* (4th edn). London: Sage Publications.

Mooney, C., Ferrie, L., Fox, S., Hansen, A. and Wrathmell, R. (2012) *Primary Mathematics: Knowledge and Understanding* (6th edn). London: Learning Matters/SAGE.

QCA (1999) *Teaching Written Calculations: Guidance for Teachers at Key Stages 1 and 2*. Sudbury: QCA Publications.

QCA (1999) *Teaching Mental Calculation Strategies: Guidance for Teachers at Key Stages 1 and 2*. Sudbury: QCA Publications.

Answers

Introduction

1. Teachers should provide children with opportunities to develop their understanding of place value throughout KS2. In particular this applies to the teaching of decimals because without an understanding of place value in the context of decimals children will not be able to calculate accurately and efficiently. Consider the child who thinks that 7.23 ('seven point twenty-three') is bigger than 7.4 because 23 is bigger than 4. Or the child who calculates 3.6 + 1.52 and gives the answer 4.58 (can you spot how the answer has been derived?). These two examples demonstrate the crucial importance of understanding place value in relation to all types of numbers, not just integers.

2. Yes, calculations involving fractions can be challenging, but one of the reasons is that children do not possess a conceptual understanding of what a fraction actually is. Children are not going to be able to calculate with fractions if they do not have a secure grasp of things such as 'equal parts' and 'equivalent fractions' or if they have no sense of size and order in relation to fractions. These are prerequisites for calculating with fractions and the foundations must be laid from KS1 onwards.

3. The guiding principles for calculations involving fractions, decimals, percentages and ratios should be the same as those involving whole numbers. Children should still ask themselves the question 'Can I do it mentally?' before considering a written approach. Indeed there may be some answers that are known as facts that can be recalled instantly – for example, when asked 'What is half of a half?' or 'What is three-quarters as a percentage?' If a written method is used then it doesn't necessarily have to be a traditional one. For example an empty number line could be used to calculate 5.1 – 3.85 by counting on in steps from the lower to the higher number.

4. Ratio and proportion are different concepts, although both are concerned with the parts that make up a whole. A ratio compares part with part – for example, we might state that the ratio of sand to cement in a mortar mixture is 4:1, in other words: four parts sand for every one part cement. A proportion compares each of the parts that make up the whole with the whole itself. So in relation to the mortar mix we can state that four-fifths is sand and one-fifth is cement. Proportions can be expressed as fractions, percentages or decimals.

5. A percentage is a fraction with a denominator of 100 and so percentages should be introduced to children as a natural extension of their understanding of fractions, using the same sorts of language, terminology, visual aids and practical resources.

6. Following on from what has been discussed in the first five questions it should be apparent that models and images are essential when teaching fractions, decimals, percentages and ratios. For example, these can be used effectively to develop children's understanding of what fractions and percentages are, to compare and

order fractions, to model early pencil-and-paper methods (e.g. using an empty number line) and to provide a visual representation of the parts that make up the whole when considering ratios.

Section 1: calculating with fractions

7. (a) The grid comprises 12 squares. A total of 4 squares are shaded. The fraction shaded is therefore $\frac{4}{12}$ which can be simplified to $\frac{1}{3}$.

   (b) $\frac{25}{35}$ of the children stop for lunch. This fraction can be simplified to $\frac{5}{7}$ (divide both the numerator and denominator by 5).

   (c) 12 out of 32 are boys, which is $\frac{12}{32}$ as a fraction. This can be simplified to $\frac{3}{8}$.

8. It is difficult to order fractions that have different denominators, so each one needs to be changed to an equivalent fraction, such that they all have the same denominator. This is called a 'common denominator'. Each of the fractions can be changed so that the denominator is 24, as follows:

$$\frac{3}{4} = \frac{18}{24}$$

$$\frac{2}{3} = \frac{16}{24}$$

$$\frac{7}{12} = \frac{14}{24}$$

$$\frac{5}{8} = \frac{15}{24}$$

The fractions can now be compared easily. The correct order is:

$$\frac{7}{12} \qquad \frac{5}{8} \qquad \frac{2}{3} \qquad \frac{3}{4}$$

An alternative approach would be to convert each fraction to a decimal, by dividing the numerator by the denominator, using a calculator where appropriate. As decimals, the four original fractions would be written as:

$$0.75 \qquad 0.667 \qquad 0.583 \qquad 0.625$$

and can now be ordered easily.

9. One-third and one-quarter cannot be compared or combined easily because they have different denominators, so each needs to be changed to an equivalent fraction

so that they have a common denominator (also see question 8 above). Each can be changed so that the denominator is 12, as shown below:

$$\frac{1}{3} = \frac{4}{12}$$

$$\frac{1}{4} = \frac{3}{12}$$

Combining these two fractions gives $\frac{7}{12}$ which means that the remaining $\frac{5}{12}$ of the children must go home for lunch.

10. (a) Calculate one-fifth of 900 kg by dividing by 5. The answer is 180 kg.

   (b) Calculate three-quarters of £75 by first dividing by 4 to find one-quarter and then multiplying by 3 to find three-quarters. The answer is £56.25.

   (c) Calculate five-eighths of 144 km by first dividing by 8 to find one-eighth and then multiplying by 5 to find five-eighths. The answer is 90 km.

11. (a) $\frac{5}{6} - \frac{1}{3} = \frac{5}{6} - \frac{2}{6} = \frac{3}{6} = \frac{1}{2}$;

   (b) $1\frac{3}{8} + 3\frac{1}{2} = 1\frac{3}{8} + 3\frac{4}{8} = 4\frac{7}{8}$;

   (c) $1\frac{3}{4} + 2\frac{2}{3} = 1\frac{9}{12} + 2\frac{8}{12} = 3\frac{17}{12} = 4\frac{5}{12}$.

12. (a) $3 \times \frac{3}{4} = \frac{9}{4} = 2\frac{1}{4}$;

   (b) $1\frac{5}{8} \times 2 = 2\frac{10}{8} = 3\frac{2}{8} = 3\frac{1}{4}$;

   (c) $\frac{3}{4} \times \frac{2}{5} = \frac{6}{20} = \frac{3}{10}$.

13. (a) $\frac{3}{4} \div 2 = \frac{3}{8}$;

   (b) $2\frac{2}{5} \div 3 = \frac{12}{5} \div 3 = \frac{4}{5}$;

   (c) $1\frac{2}{3} \div 4 = \frac{5}{3} \div 4 = \frac{5}{12}$.

Section 2: calculating with decimals

14. (a) 0.001   0.01   0.09   0.1   0.11   0.99

   It is helpful to write them so that they all have the same number of decimal places – i.e. 3 decimal places (thousandths) in this particular example:

$$0.001 \qquad 0.010 \qquad 0.090 \qquad 0.100 \qquad 0.110 \qquad 0.990$$

(b) The first two on the list above (0.001 and 0.01) are the closest because they have a difference of only 9 thousandths (0.009). The differences, in thousandths, between other adjacent pairs in the list are 80, 10, 10 and 880 respectively.

(c) The two that have a sum of 1 are 0.99 and 0.01.

15. (a) $4.65 + 1.2 + 0.35 = 6.2$.

Efficient method: look for numbers that can be added easily – i.e. $4.65 + 0.35 = 5$.

(b) $10.1 - 9.85 = 0.25$.

Efficient method: the two numbers are close together so count up from the lower to the higher, passing 10 on the way. From 9.85 to 10 is a step of 0.15 and from 10 to 10.1 is a step of 0.1. Alternatively, think in terms of money – i.e. 'I've got £10.10 and spend £9.85. How much will I have left?

(c) $7.89 \times 3 = 23.67$.

Efficient method: 7.89 is close to 8, so work out 8×3 and subtract 3 lots of 0.11. $24 - 0.33 = 23.67$.

(d) $2.75 \div 0.25 = 11$.

Efficient method: think in terms of 'How many lots of 0.25 can I get from 2.75?' There are 4 lots of 0.25 in 1, so there are 8 lots in 2, plus 3 lots in 0.75. You could also think in terms of money – i.e. 'How many items costing 25p each can I get with £2.75?'

The key point to note from the solutions above is that all the efficient mental methods discussed in Chapter 2 in relation to whole numbers can be applied equally to decimals. Even with decimals, mental methods should always be seen as the first resort.

16. (a) $13.8 + 5.326 = 19.126$.

This could be tackled using the traditional written method for addition, with the numbers set out in columns, underneath one another as shown below (see Chapter 4). It is crucially important that the numbers are positioned correctly, so that the tens are aligned with the tens, the ones with the ones, the tenths with the tenths, and so on.

$$
\begin{array}{r}
13.8 \\
+ \quad 5_1.326 \\
\hline
19.126
\end{array}
$$

(b) $9.4 - 6.18 = 3.22$.

This could be tackled using the traditional written method of subtraction by decomposition (see Chapter 4). As in (a) above, the digits must be aligned correctly. It is also helpful to fill any 'gaps' after the decimal points with zeros, as is the case with 9.40 below:

$$9.\ ^{3}\!\!\not{4}\ ^{1}0$$
$$-\ \underline{6.\ \ 1\ \ 8}$$
$$\underline{3.\ \ 2\ \ 2}$$

It could also be tackled using an informal written method, counting on from the lower to the higher number and recording the steps (see Chapter 3), as shown below:

6.18

$(+0.82)$

7

$(+2.4)$

9.4

(Total 3.22)

(c) $58.6 \times 2.4 = 140.64$.

This can be tackled using the traditional written method of long multiplication (see Chapter 4). The recommended procedure is to ignore any decimal points and therefore calculate 586×24. The decimal point is inserted in the answer by estimating.

$$
\begin{array}{r}
5\ 8\ 6 \\
\times\ \ _{1\,1\,3\,2}2\ 4 \\
\hline
2\ 3\ 4\ 4 \\
1\,1{,}7\ 2\ 0 \\
\hline
1\ 4\ 0\ 6\ 4
\end{array}
$$

A rough estimate of 58.6×2.4 is $60 \times 2 = 120$, so the correct answer must be 140.64 because it could not possibly be 1.4064 or 1406.4 or 14064. An alternative to the traditional method would be to use the grid method to calculate 586×24 (see Chapter 3) and again use estimation to insert the decimal point in the answer.

(d) $24.36 \div 7 = 3.48$.

This can be tackled using the traditional written method of short division (see Chapter 4). The decimal point in the answer should be aligned with the decimal point in 24.36, although an alternative approach would be to ignore the decimal points completely and then insert one in the answer by estimating.

$$
\begin{array}{r}
3.\ 4\ 8 \\
\hline
7\,)\overline{2\ 4.^{3}3^{5}6}
\end{array}
$$

Section 3: calculating with percentages

17. (a) The grid comprises 16 squares. 12 squares are shaded. The fraction shaded is therefore $\dfrac{12}{16}$ which can be simplified to $\dfrac{3}{4}$. As a percentage $\dfrac{3}{4}$ is 75%.

(b) As a fraction the test score is $\dfrac{17}{20}$, which can be converted to the equivalent fraction $\dfrac{85}{100}$ (multiply both the numerator and denominator by 5). As a percentage $\dfrac{85}{100}$ is 85%.

(c) There are 120 children altogether, of whom 75 stop for lunch. As a fraction this is $\dfrac{75}{120}$, which can be simplified to give $\dfrac{5}{8}$. As a percentage $\dfrac{5}{8}$ is 62.5%.

18. (a) 100% of £250 = £250

      50% of £250 = £125   (divide £250 by 2)

      25% of £250 = £62.50 (divide £125 by 2)

      75% of £250 = £187.50 (add 50% (£125) and 25% (£62.50))

   (b) 100% of £120 = £120

      10% of £120 = £12   (divide £120 by 10)

      5% of £120 = £6   (divide £12 by 2)

      30% of £120 = £36   (multiply £12 by 3)

      35% of £120 = £42   (add 30% (£36) and 5% (£6))

   (c) 100% of £48 = £48

      10% of £48 = £4.80   (divide £48 by 10)

      5% of £48 = £2.40   (divide £4.80 by 2)

      2½% of £48 = £1.20   (divide £2.40 by 2)

      17½% of £48 = £8.40   (add 10% (£4.80), 5% (£2.40) and 2½% (£1.20))

19. (a) 100% of £380 = £380

      10% of £380 = £38   (divide £380 by 10)

      5% of £380 = £19   (divide £38 by 2)

      105% of £380 = £399   (add 100% (£380) and 5% (£19) to give the final wage)

   (b) 100% of £85 = £85

      10% of £85 = £8.50   (divide £85 by 10)

      20% of £85 = £17   (multiply £8.50 by 2)

      80% of £85 = £68   (either subtract 20% (£17) from 100% (£85) or multiply 20% (£17) by 4 to give the sale price)

   (c) 100% of £56 = £56

      10% of £56 = £5.60   (divide £56 by 10)

      5% of £380 = £2.80   (divide £5.60 by 2)

      15% of £56 = £8.40   (add 10% (£5.60) and 5% (£2.80) to give the service charge)

      115% of £56 = £64.40   (add 100% (£56) and 15% (£8.40) to give the final cost)

20. The bicycle has been reduced by 25% so the sale price, £270, represents 75% of the original price:

    75% of original price = £270

    25% of original price = £90 (divide £270 by 3)

    100% of original price = £360 (multiply £90 by 4 to give the original price)

    You can check the answer by reducing £360 by 25% to see if this gives the correct sale price of £270.

21. The final price of £174 is the pre-VAT price (100%), plus 20% VAT, so it is 120% of the pre-VAT price:

    120% of pre-VAT price = £174

    20% of pre-VAT price = £29 (divide £174 by 6)

    100% of pre-VAT price = £145 (multiply £29 by 5 to give the pre-VAT price)

    You can check the answer by increasing £145 by 20% to see if this gives the correct final price of £174.

Section 4: calculating with ratios

22. (a)   Boys to girls

                12 :   20

                 3 :   5 (simplify the ratio by dividing both numbers by 4)

    The ratio of boys to girls is 3:5.

    (b)   Grey to white

                 4 : 8

                 1 : 2 (simplify the ratio by dividing both numbers by 4)

    The ratio of grey to white is 1:2.

    (c)   School to home

                25 : 10

                 5 : 2 (simplify the ratio by dividing both numbers by 5)

    The ratio of school dinners to home dinners is 5:2.

    You might like to compare the questions and responses here to those presented in question 7 earlier in this chapter. They refer to the same three scenarios, but question 7 considers them in terms of fractions and question 22 in terms of ratios. This illustrates the distinction between ratio (question 22) and proportion (question 7).

23. (a)   Strawberries to sugar

                 3 : 4

                12 : 16 (scale up the ratio by multiplying both numbers by 4)

    With 12 kg of strawberries you need 16 kg of sugar.

(b) Strawberries to sugar

$$3 \quad : \quad 4 \text{ (difference between strawberries and sugar is 1)}$$

$$27 \quad : \quad 36 \text{ (we want a difference of 9, so scale up by a factor of 9)}$$

You will need 27 kg of strawberries and 36 kg of sugar.

(c) Strawberries to sugar

$$3 \quad : \quad 4$$

$$0.75 \quad : \quad 1 \text{ (scale down by a factor of 4)}$$

$$15 \times 0.75 \quad : \quad 15 \text{ (scale up by a factor of 15)}$$

$$11.25 \quad : \quad 15$$

With 15 kg of sugar you need 11.25 kg of strawberries.

24. (a) Map to land

$$1 \quad : \quad 500,000$$

$$1 \text{ cm} \quad : \quad 500,000 \text{ cm}$$

$$1 \text{ cm} \quad : \quad 5000 \text{ m (convert to land distance to metres)}$$

$$1 \text{ cm} \quad : \quad 5 \text{ km (convert to land distance to kilometres)}$$

$$2.5 \text{ cm} \quad : \quad 12.5 \text{ km (scale up by a factor of 2.5)}$$

The distance between the two villages is 12.5 km.

(b) Map to land

$$1 \text{ cm} \quad : \quad 5 \text{ km (we already know this from part (a))}$$

$$0.2 \text{ cm} \quad : \quad 1 \text{ km (scale down by a factor of 5)}$$

$$5.6 \text{ cm} \quad : \quad 28 \text{ km (scale up by a factor of 28)}$$

The distance between the two towns on the map is 5.6 cm.

25. This question provides an opportunity to demonstrate the distinction between ratio and proportion. As a ratio the ingredients flour, sugar and butter are mixed in the ratio 4:1:3, but as proportions we can say that $\frac{4}{8}$ is flour, $\frac{1}{8}$ is sugar and $\frac{3}{8}$ is butter. As well as being written as fractions, these proportions can be written as percentages (50%, 12.5%, 37.5%) and decimals (0.5, 0.125, 0.375).

If the total weight of mixture is 1 kg (1000 g) then:

50% is flour, which is 500 g

12.5% is sugar, which is 125 g

32.5% is butter, which is 375 g

6 Calculation using technology

> ### Learning outcomes
>
> This chapter will help you to:
>
> - understand some of the general issues associated with the use of technology in the teaching of calculation;
> - audit your knowledge, skills and understanding in relation to both the technical and the pedagogical aspects of using technology;
> - identify resources to further develop your knowledge, skills and understanding in relation to the use of technology in the teaching of calculation.

Introduction

Before auditing your knowledge, skills and understanding in relation to the use of technology for calculation, let us first consider a few general issues in relation to this subject.

Agree/disagree

Read the following statements and decide whether you agree or disagree with each one. Then compare your thoughts with the notes provided at the end of the chapter.

1. The National Curriculum programmes of study for mathematics provide detailed guidance regarding the role of technology in the teaching and learning of mathematics.

2. Giving primary-age children easy access to a calculator will have an adverse effect on the development of their mental calculation skills.

3. Children should not be allowed to use calculators until they know their addition and subtraction facts for numbers up to 20 and their multiplication facts up to 12×12.

4. There is no reason why a teacher would want to use a calculator with children until they are in year 6.

Section 1: using a calculator

Answer each of the following questions and then compare your responses with those provided at the end of the chapter.

5. Without using a calculator, work out the answer to the following calculation:

$$4 + 5 \times 6 =$$

If a child were asked to carry out the same calculation, what possible answers might he or she come up with? Use a calculator to work out the answer and compare this to your responses above. Try using different calculators. Do they all give the same answer?

6. A group of seven people go out for a meal. The bill is £156.96 and they share the cost equally. Use a calculator to work out how much each person pays.

7. A school collects supermarket vouchers to exchange for books. Each book requires 435 vouchers. Use a calculator to work out how many books can be claimed if 23,479 vouchers have been collected.

8. Use a calculator to work out the sum of all the square numbers between 500 and 800 without writing down any of the intermediate answers.

9. Use a calculator to work out the answer to the following calculation:

$$98,765,432 \div 0.00127$$

Is your calculator able to display the answer? Do you understand what is being displayed?

10. Five small pizzas are shared equally between 3 people. How much does each person get? Why would it be inappropriate to use a calculator to give a decimal answer to this question?

11. Use a calculator to work out the answer to the following calculation:

$$5 \div 0$$

Is your calculator able to display the answer? Do you understand why you are getting this in the display? If a child asked you what the answer to $5 \div 0$ is, what would be your response?

12. (a) A cube has a volume of 2500 cm³. Use a calculator to work out the length of each side of the cube. You should only use the basic four arithmetical operators – i.e. do not use the cube root facility if you have got a scientific calculator. Give your answer correct to two decimal places.
    (b) Use a calculator to work out the answer to $5.42 \div 1.25$, but without using the division key.
    (c) Use a calculator to work out the answer to 2.375×5.7, but without using the multiplication key.

Section 2: calculation with a spreadsheet

Answer each of the following questions and then compare your responses with those provided at the end of the chapter.

13. Create a spreadsheet to model this scenario and answer the questions. A cook has a 1 kg bag of flour. On day one she uses half of the flour. On day two she uses half of what is

left. On day three she uses half of what is left. She continues in this way, each day using half of the flour that is available. How much flour will she have used altogether by the end of the 10th day (to the nearest gram)? If she continues in the same way for many days, how much flour will she have eventually used up altogether?

Another cook starts with a 1 kg of flour but she uses a third of what she has got each day. How much of the flour will she eventually use? What about the cook who uses a quarter of her flour each day?

14. Here is a well known mathematical number sequence:

1, 1, 2, 3, 5, 8, 13, 21, 34, 55, 89…

What is the name of this number sequence? Can you see how the sequence is generated?

Create a spreadsheet to generate this sequence. The first two numbers can be typed, but all subsequent numbers must be produced by a single formula that can then be copied into other cells.

In an adjacent row or column of the spreadsheet use a formula to investigate the ratios of consecutive numbers in the sequence. In other words, divide the 2nd number by the 1st, the 3rd by the 2nd, the 4th by the 3rd, and so on. What do you notice about these ratios?

15. Create a spreadsheet to model this scenario and answer the questions. On 1 January you receive 1p, on 2 January you receive 2p, on 3 January you receive 4p, on 4 January you receive 8p, and so on like that for the rest of the month. How much will you receive on 31 January? How much will you have received in total during the month?

16. If the scenario described in question 15 were to be extended to the end of February, the amount received might be displayed on the spreadsheet something like this:

$$2.8833E+15$$

What does this mean? What is the number being displayed?

What to do next?

Developing your own subject knowledge

If your knowledge and understanding of how technology can be used to teach calculation are in need of further development, it is recommended that you read *Teaching Arithmetic in Primary Schools*, Chapter 7 ('Arithmetic using technology'). This chapter provides:

- a detailed discussion of the research and inspection evidence associated with the use of calculators in primary schools;

- worked examples and case studies to illustrate some of the technical aspects of using calculators, such as the memory facility and the constant function;

- step-by-step instructions to help you to understand the different sorts of formulae and built-in functions that can be used on a spreadsheet;

- suggestions for activities that you can use in the classroom which make use of technology.

Another valuable book to consider looking at is *Maths and ICT in the Primary School: A Creative Approach*. There is a whole chapter devoted to the creative use of calculators and you will also find several sections throughout the book that consider the use of spreadsheets from both the teacher's perspective and that of the pupils. Also consider *Understanding and Teaching Primary Mathematics*, Chapter 12 ('ICT and teaching and learning mathematics').

The examples in this chapter may have highlighted gaps in your subject knowledge that do not necessarily relate directly to the use of technology. If you are still unsure about scientific notation or standard form, you can find out more about this in any of the following sources:

- *The Primary Teacher's Guide to Number*, Chapter 1 ('The structure and language of number').

- *Primary Mathematics: Knowledge and Understanding*, Chapter 2 ('Number').

- *Mathematics Explained for Primary Teachers*, Chapter 18 ('Calculations with decimals').

- For a more detailed discussion of division by zero, see *The Primary Teacher's Guide to Number*, Chapter 2 ('Calculations') and to find out more about the Fibonacci sequence and the Golden Ratio, see Chapter 3 of the same book ('Fractions, decimals, percentages and ratios').

Developing your knowledge of the curriculum

As discussed elsewhere in this chapter, the guidance provided in the National Curriculum programmes of study for mathematics regarding the use of technology is minimal and so you will have to look elsewhere to find out about the typical expectations being placed upon staff and children. Read the mathematics schemes of work in your placement schools and in particular try to identify the ways in which staff and children are recommended to utilise technology. Also speak to staff in your placement schools to ascertain their views on the use of technology in the teaching of mathematics.

Recommended reading

Cotton, T. (2010) *Understanding and Teaching Primary Mathematics*. Harlow: Pearson Education.

English, R. (2006) *Maths and ICT in the Primary School: A Creative Approach*. London: David Fulton Publishers.

English, R. (2012) *The Primary Teacher's Guide to Number*. Whitney: Scholastic.

English, R. (2013) *Teaching Arithmetic in Primary Schools*. London: Learning Matters/ SAGE.

Haylock, D. (2010) *Mathematics Explained for Primary Teachers* (4th edn). London: Sage Publications.

Mooney, C., Ferrie, L., Fox, S., Hansen, A. and Wrathmell, R. (2012) *Primary Mathematics: Knowledge and Understanding* (6th edn). London: Learning Matters/SAGE.

Answers

Introduction

1. The latest version of the National Curriculum programmes of study for mathematics provides very little guidance with regard to the role of technology. In the actual programmes of study for upper Key Stage 2 there are a few very brief mentions of ICT tools in relation to geometry and data, but nothing else. In the introduction to the programmes of study it merely states that 'teachers should use their judgement about when ICT tools should be used.'

2. If calculators are used appropriately with children in primary schools, there is no reason at all why they should have an adverse effect on the development of mental skills. Teachers must ensure that children do not use a calculator for simple calculations that can be tackled mentally, but should do this by promoting mental skills as being something to be proud of. Children's poor mental skills are more likely to be the result of poor teaching and a lack of emphasis on developing these skills than exposure to calculators.

3. As stated above, a calculator should not be used as a substitute for mental skills, but at the same time we need to recognise that it has the potential to be much more than a calculating device. By thinking creatively you can devise opportunities to use calculators to support teaching and learning in many ways, some of which actually contribute to the learning of number facts. For example, utilising the constant function turns a calculator into a counting machine which encourages children to count on mentally and become familiar with multiples and multiplication facts (press 3 + = = = = and see what happens).

4. Calculators do have a significant role to play in upper Key Stage 2 when children are exploring bigger and more complex numbers, but this does not imply that they cannot be used effectively with younger children, as illustrated by the following examples:

   - Young children will encounter digital displays in their everyday lives and so teachers need to prepare them for this unique way of presenting numbers. A calculator is an ideal tool for this.

   - The constant function (press 1 + = = = =) can be used to reinforce the ordering and sequencing of numbers.

- As well as counting up in 1s, the constant function can also be used to count up or down in any step. Try $100 - 5 = = = =$ or $7 + = = = =$. This assists the development of mental addition and subtraction, the learning of multiples and the exploration of digit patterns in the multiplication tables.

- A calculator can be used to reinforce aspects of place value – for example by displaying 853 and asking a child what needs to be subtracted in order to replace the 5 with a zero.

- A calculator can encourage children to think about the relationships between numbers and operations – for example by asking a child to find a way of calculating 525×37 without pressing the 5 key.

- Activities whose main focus is problem-solving, as opposed to manual calculation, are often best carried out with the aid of a calculator – for example by asking a child to find two numbers with a sum of 100 and a product of 2356.

- A calculator can be a source of numbers to use to reinforce rounding skills – for example to the nearest 10, nearest 100 or nearest whole number.

Section 1: using a calculator

5. You and the children may have come up with two possible answers: 34 and 54, depending on the order in which the calculations were carried out. Strictly speaking, mathematical convention dictates that the multiplication should be carried out before the addition, giving the answer 34, although the best way to avoid any confusion is to use brackets to denote precedence, as shown below:

$$(4 + 5) \times 6 = 54$$

$$4 + (5 \times 6) = 34$$

In terms of calculator use, the important thing to be aware of is the fact that different calculators give different answers to calculations like the one presented in this question, due to the way that they have been programmed to deal with operation precedence.

6. The correct answer is £22.43 per person. The calculator will display the answer 22.4228571 and so it would be tempting to round this to the nearest penny to give £22.42 per person. However, if they each pay £22.42 this will give a total of £156.94, which will not cover the bill. In terms of your own subject knowledge and implications for your teaching, there are two important points raised by this question:

- When using a calculator to solve problems involving money, answers usually have to be rounded to the nearest penny.

- In any problem-solving situation the final answer must take account of the context in which the problem is set. For example, in this particular question the context dictated that it was appropriate to round up rather than down.

You must ensure that you provide children with opportunities to develop these sorts of problem-solving skills.

7. The correct answer is 53 books. The calculator will display the answer 53.9747126 which you might have rounded to the nearest whole number to give the answer 54 books. However, there are not enough vouchers to exchange for 54 books – the school is 11 vouchers short of the requirement. This example raises similar points to those raised in the previous one – that is, the importance of the context in which a problem is set and the need to provide children with opportunities to develop the necessary skills.

8. The answer is 3919, derived by adding the following square numbers:

$$529 \quad 576 \quad 625 \quad 676 \quad 729 \quad 784$$

The key subject-knowledge issue raised by this question is your ability to use the calculator's memory facility. Even the most basic calculators have this facility, but most people rarely use it because they do not know how to. It is therefore vitally important that you know how to use it yourself so that you can teach these skills to the children.

9. Unless your calculator display is able to accommodate many digits, it is unlikely that you have obtained a straightforward answer, because the whole number part alone extends to 11 digits. It is therefore likely that your calculator displayed one of the following:

An error message

7.7768057 10 (note the space before the last two digits)

7.7768057 **E10**

7.7768057 **E+10**

The number of decimal places may be truncated depending on the space available. For example you might see **7.7768 E10**. All these are examples of what is called *scientific notation* or *standard form*. In terms of your own subject knowledge it is important that you understand this notation and are able to interpret the calculator display. In relation to this specific example the number displayed is $7.7768057 \times 10^{10} = 77,768,057,000$. This number is given correct to 8 significant figures, due to space restrictions in the display.

10. The correct answer is $1\frac{2}{3}$ pizzas for each person. You could use a calculator to find the answer, as follows:

$$5 \div 3 = 1.6666667$$

When presenting the answer you would probably round it to two or three decimal places and so state that it is 1.667 pizzas for each person. However, now multiply the answer by 3 and see what you get:

$$1.667 \times 3 = 5.001$$

Where did the extra one-thousandth of a pizza come from? It is because the final digit has been rounded up to 7. So why not use the answer as 1.666 as shown below:

$$1.666 \times 3 = 4.998$$

Now we seem to have lost two-thousandths of a pizza!

In terms of your own subject knowledge you need to understand that when using decimals it is sometimes not possible to give precise answers and so it is therefore more appropriate to use fractions, which can be used in a more precise way.

11. The calculator has probably displayed an error message of some sort because it is not possible to display the answer to $5 \div 0$ in numerical terms. When we divide by zero the result is considered to be *infinite* or *undefined*. Use a calculator to divide 5 by numbers that are smaller and smaller each time. For example, divide 5 by 1, then by 0.1, then by 0.01, then by 0.001, then by 0.0001, and so on. The answers that you get should give you some understanding of why dividing by zero gives an infinitely large answer.

12. (a) The length of the sides is 13.57 cm. In order to calculate this you probably employed trial and improvement skills, as well as estimation skills. You also need to understand place value in the context of decimals The early stages of your working out may have looked something like this:

$$12^3 = 1728 \text{ (too small)}$$

$$13^3 = 2197 \text{ (too small)}$$

$$14^3 = 2744 \text{ (too big)}$$

$$13.5^3 = 2460.375 \text{ (too small)}$$

$$13.6^3 = 2515.456 \text{ (too big)}$$

(b) The answer is 4.336. In order to calculate the answer without pressing the division key you first need to understand the inverse relationship between multiplication and division, and then you must employ trial and improvement skills and estimation skills, similar to those in part (a) above. The first stage is explained below, with the letter A being used to represent the answer that we are trying to establish.

$$\text{If } 5.42 \div 1.25 = A$$

$$\text{then } A \times 1.25 = 5.42$$

Now use trial and improvement methods to find A, using the multiplication key on the calculator.

(c) The answer is 13.5375. You could adopt a similar approach to that used in part (b) above, based on inverse relationships, to produce two possible division equations, as shown below:

If $2.375 \times 5.7 = A$

then $A \div 5.7 = 2.375$

and $A \div 2.375 = 5.7$

A completely different approach would be to recognise that 2.375 lots of 5.7 can be thought of as 2 lots of 5.7 plus 0.375 lots of 5.7 and then use repeated addition to work out each answer. Essentially we are partitioning 2.375 into whole numbers and decimals and then utilising the distributive law. The 2 lots of 5.7 is a straightforward addition (or why not just add 5.7 to the memory twice?). The 0.375 lots of 5.7 utilises your understanding of fractions and decimals because, as you know, 0.375 is three-eighths. You can calculate one-eighth of 5.7 by dividing by 8 and then use repeated addition to find three-eighths (or just add one-eighth to the memory three times). A variation on the second approach above is to think of 5.7 lots of 2.375 as 5 lots of 2.375 plus 0.7 lots of 2.375. You could also think of it as 6 lots of 2.375 less 0.3 lots of 2.375.

These three examples illustrate that a calculator is a valuable tool to support teaching and learning. You might like to think about possible learning objectives for lessons that incorporate activities like the three presented above. The objectives are likely to focus on things such as trial and improvement, estimation, place value, partitioning, inverse operations, and so on.

Section 2: calculation with a spreadsheet

13. By the end of the 10th day she will have used 999 grams altogether. Eventually she will, to all intents and purposes, use all of the flour, although in theory there will always be an infinitely small amount remaining each day. The cook who uses a third of what she has got each day will eventually use half the flour. The cook who uses a quarter of what she has got each day will eventually use a third of the flour.

If you struggled to create the spreadsheet, here are a few tips to get you started for the first cook's scenario:

In cell A1 type the number **1000**

In cell A2 type the formula =**A1/2**

Copy this formula down the column as far as row 20. Column A will display the amount of flour used each day.

To find the total for the first 10 days, type the following formula into an adjacent cell – for example into cell C1:

=**SUM(A2:A11)**

14. The sequence is called the Fibonacci sequence, named after the Italian mathematician Fibonacci, who was also known as Leonardo of Pisa. Each number is the sum of the previous two numbers. As you move through the sequence the ratio of consecutive numbers approaches 1.618, a number known as the Golden Ratio.

If you are still finding the spreadsheet skills a challenge, here are a few hints:

In cell A1 type the number 1

In cell A2 type the number 1

In cell A3 type the formula = **A1+A2**

Copy this formula down the column as far as row 20. Each cell should display the sum of the two numbers immediately above – i.e. the Fibonacci sequence.

In cell B2 type the formula = **A2/A1**

Copy this formula down the column as far as row 20. Each cell should display the ratio of two consecutive Fibonacci numbers.

15. On 31 January you will receive £10,737,418.24 and by the end of the month you will have received £21,474,836.47 in total.

Here are some brief instructions for writing the spreadsheet:

In cell A1 type the number 0.01

In cell A2 type the formula = **A1*2** (the asterisk is used for multiplication)

Copy this formula down the column as far as row 31. Column A will display the amount received each day in pounds.

To find the total for the first 31 days, type the following formula into an adjacent cell – for example into cell C1:

= **SUM(A1:A31)**

16. The number has been displayed using *scientific notation* or *standard form*, as discussed earlier in the response to question 9. The number is:

$$2.8833 \times 10^{15} = 2,883,300,000,000,000$$

This number has been displayed correct to 5 significant figures.

Appendix 1

Here are three sets of 25 questions related to addition and subtraction facts up to 20 (a National Curriculum requirement for children in year 2). Use each set to test yourself by jotting down the answers to all the questions and doing it against the clock. Make a note of how long it takes you to complete a set. You will find the answers on page 17. You should be aiming for a near-perfect score and a time under 1 minute (that's about 2 seconds per question).

Set 1	
1.	4 + 6
2.	19 − 11
3.	17 − 4
4.	8 + 13
5.	11 − 6
6.	15 − 9
7.	8 + 3
8.	20 + 90
9.	15 + 6
10.	300 + 200
11.	18 − 13
12.	20 + 140
13.	13 + 4
14.	100 − 60
15.	18 − 9
16.	60 + 70
17.	7 + 18
18.	17 − 11
19.	50 + 80
20.	900 − 200
21.	2 + 19
22.	30 + 60
23.	16 − 9
24.	4 + 12
25.	3 + 19

Set 2	
1.	5 + 10
2.	13 + 15
3.	16 − 11
4.	30 + 80
5.	18 − 13
6.	12 + 7
7.	150 − 70
8.	2 + 19
9.	80 + 40
10.	7 + 17
11.	15 − 9
12.	17 − 6
13.	40 + 20
14.	17 + 5
15.	6 + 8
16.	50 + 140
17.	18 − 11
18.	14 + 5
19.	8 + 13
20.	15 − 7
21.	60 + 50
22.	19 − 13
23.	120 − 70
24.	300 + 600
25.	4 + 7

Set 3	
1.	5 + 8
2.	7 + 3
3.	9 + 18
4.	18 − 7
5.	6 + 16
6.	90 − 50
7.	17 + 7
8.	40 + 150
9.	800 − 500
10.	14 − 12
11.	20 + 40
12.	16 + 9
13.	9 + 17
14.	11 − 2
15.	13 + 11
16.	7 + 18
17.	16 − 8
18.	20 + 140
19.	700 − 200
20.	10 + 12
21.	20 − 13
22.	15 + 6
23.	90 + 30
24.	80 − 60
25.	8 + 13

Appendix 2

Here are three sets of 25 questions related to multiplication facts up to 12×12 (a National Curriculum requirement for children in year 4). Use each set to test yourself by jotting down the answers to all the questions and doing it against the clock. Make a note of how long it takes you to complete a set. You will find the answers on page 18. You should be aiming for a near-perfect score and a time under 1 minute (that's about 2 seconds per question).

	Set 1			Set 2			Set 3
1.	8×11		1.	7×7		1.	10×6
2.	6×4		2.	5×4		2.	2×9
3.	$72 \div 8$		3.	12×2		3.	$110 \div 10$
4.	5×6		4.	$28 \div 4$		4.	5×3
5.	12×7		5.	5×5		5.	$48 \div 6$
6.	$21 \div 3$		6.	3×9		6.	11×11
7.	4×2		7.	11×12		7.	4×6
8.	12×11		8.	$63 \div 9$		8.	$32 \div 8$
9.	$44 \div 11$		9.	8×8		9.	12×10
10.	4×9		10.	5×11		10.	9×9
11.	$54 \div 6$		11.	$32 \div 8$		11.	$45 \div 9$
12.	5×3		12.	7×5		12.	12×5
13.	7×10		13.	$48 \div 4$		13.	6×6
14.	$48 \div 12$		14.	$56 \div 7$		14.	$28 \div 7$
15.	3×9		15.	3×12		15.	11×6
16.	9×6		16.	6×4		16.	7×12
17.	$60 \div 10$		17.	$54 \div 6$		17.	$49 \div 7$
18.	$35 \div 5$		18.	7×6		18.	6×9
19.	8×7		19.	$36 \div 12$		19.	5×7
20.	10×9		20.	3×7		20.	2×11
21.	$27 \div 9$		21.	5×10		21.	$63 \div 9$
22.	12×12		22.	$24 \div 3$		22.	$36 \div 3$
23.	5×8		23.	5×9		23.	5×8
24.	$63 \div 9$		24.	$80 \div 8$		24.	4×4
25.	$18 \div 3$		25.	$18 \div 6$		25.	$24 \div 2$

Appendix 3

Final summary audit/test: 100 questions for you to try

The 100 questions in this appendix will enable you to carry out a comprehensive audit of your calculation capabilities. The questions cover all the skills and techniques presented in the book, so you could use this appendix first, as a way to check which chapters you should focus your attention on, or you could attempt this summary audit/test once you have worked through all the earlier chapters, to check your understanding.

When you have completed this summary audit/test you can check your responses by referring to Appendix 4.

Section 1: the recall of number facts

Here are 25 questions related the recall of facts for all four calculation operations. Test yourself by answering these questions against the clock. You should be aiming for a time under 1 minute (that's about 2 seconds per question).

1.	$7 + 6$	10.	$18 + 9$	18.	$15 + 8$
2.	$18 - 12$	11.	$56 \div 7$	19.	7×3
3.	4×7	12.	9×4	20.	$27 \div 3$
4.	$150 - 80$	13.	$400 + 900$	21.	$16 - 7$
5.	11×6	14.	$21 - 13$	22.	6×4
6.	$35 \div 5$	15.	8×6	23.	$90 + 50$
7.	$80 + 30$	16.	$55 \div 11$	24.	$17 - 6$
8.	$120 - 70$	17.	3×12	25.	$64 \div 8$
9.	$84 \div 12$				

Section 2: mental calculation

Mentally calculate the answer to each of the following questions. You should write down nothing apart from the answer.

1.	$79 + 53$
2.	98×6
3.	$705 - 689$
4.	$740 \div 20$
5.	27×8
6.	$48 + 65 + 32$
7.	$280 \div 5$
8.	$367 - 252$

9.	8×39
10.	$66 - 47 + 34$
11.	900×30
12.	$185 - 26 - 54$
13.	63×5
14.	$10 + 11 + 12 + 13 + 14 + 15$
15.	$488 \div 4$

Section 3: informal pencil-and-paper calculation

Calculate the answer to each of the following questions. Feel free to write down any working out that you need, but you should not use any of the traditional compact pencil-and-paper methods. This will enable you to practise and demonstrate competence using informal pencil-and-paper approaches. In the case of the division questions, if the answer is not an exact whole number give your answer using remainders.

1.	$287 + 456$
2.	$863 - 572$
3.	743×6
4.	$238 \div 14$
5.	376×13

6.	$508 + 134$
7.	$829 \div 43$
8.	$2087 - 805$
9.	613×32
10.	$1135 \div 26$

Section 4: traditional pencil-and-paper calculation

Calculate the answer to each of the following questions using the traditional compact pencil-and-paper methods. In the case of the division questions, if the answer is not an exact whole number give your answer using remainders.

1.	$373 + 509$
2.	$925 - 476$
3.	4273×9
4.	$598 \div 7$
5.	$3017 - 1463$

6.	$1489 + 345 + 217$
7.	419×51
8.	$3750 \div 18$
9.	3059×37
10.	$6000 \div 55$

Section 5: calculation with fractions

You should not use a calculator when answering any of the questions in this section.

Here are four fractions:

$$\frac{3}{4} \qquad \frac{2}{3} \qquad \frac{7}{12} \qquad \frac{5}{8}$$

1. Which one is equivalent to $\dfrac{8}{12}$?

2. Which one is the smallest?

3. Which one is the biggest?

4. What is the sum of the two biggest fractions?

5. What is the difference between the two smallest fractions?

6. What is the product of the two biggest fractions?

7. What is half of the biggest fraction?

8. Work out three-quarters of £125.

9. A man earns £350 each week. He spends £140 on rent. What fraction of his wages is spent on rent?

10. A litre is approximately 1¾ pints. How many pints is 5 litres?

Section 6: calculation with decimals

You should not use a calculator when answering any of the questions in this section.

Here are four decimal numbers:

3.09   3.105   3.1   3.089

1. Which one is the smallest?

2. Which one is the biggest?

3. Which two are closest to one another?

4. Which two numbers have a difference of one-hundredth $\left(\dfrac{1}{100}\right)$?

5. What is the sum of the two smallest numbers?

6. What is the difference between the biggest and the smallest numbers?

7. Multiply the smallest number by 7.

8. What is the product of the two numbers with the fewest digits?

9. Work out half of the smallest number.

10. Divide the biggest number by 3.

Section 7: calculation with percentages

You should not use a calculator when answering any of the questions in this section.

1. A child scores 19 out of 25 in a test. What is the child's percentage score?

2. In a class there are 18 boys and 22 girls. What percentage of the class is boys?

3. What is five-eighths as a percentage?

4. What is 30% of £250?

5. What is 75% of £140?

6. A meal costs £90 plus a 12.5% service charge. What is the total cost of the meal?

7. The original price of a coat is £80. The price is reduced by 25% in the sale. The sale price is reduced by 15% in the blue-cross sale. What is the blue-cross sale price?

8. The price of a jacket is reduced by 20% in the sale. The sale price is £28. What was the original price?

Section 8: calculation with ratios

You should not use a calculator when answering any of the questions in this section.

1. In June it rained on 6 days and it was dry for the rest of the month. What is the ratio of rainy days to dry days?

2. Two-fifths of the children in a class are boys. What is the ratio of boys to girls?

3. Mortar requires sand and cement to be mixed in the ratio 7:3. What percentage of the mixture is cement?

4. A builder mixes mortar as described above. He uses 15 kg cement. How much sand docs he use?

5. A recipe requires flour and sugar to be mixed in the ratio 5:2. A cook uses 90 g more flour than sugar. How much flour and how much sugar does he use?

6. On another occasion the cook uses the same recipe described above, but this time the total weight of the mixture is 350 g. How much flour and how much sugar does he use?

Section 9: calculation with a calculator

1. Use a calculator to work out the sum of all the square numbers between 750 and 1000 without writing down any of the intermediate answers.

2. Use a calculator to work out the square root of 150, but without using the square root key. Give your answer correct to 3 decimal places.

3. Use a calculator to work out the answer to 3.65×4.2, but without using the multiplication key.

4. Use a calculator to work out the answer to $8.34 \div 1.5$, but without using the division key.

5. Use a calculator to work out the answer to 2.19×11.7, but without using the decimal point key.

6. You put £500 in a savings account on 1 January. 8% interest is added to the balance on 31 December each year. How long does it take for your investment to double in value?

Appendix 4

Final summary audit/test: answers

Here are the answers to the 100 questions in Appendix 3. Only the answers are provided. If you have got a question wrong and would like further guidance on possible arithmetical approaches, please see the relevant chapter in this book.

Section 1: the recall of number facts

For further guidance, please see Chapter 2.

1.	13	10.	27	18.	23
2.	6	11.	8	19.	21
3.	28	12.	36	20.	9
4.	70	13.	1300	21.	9
5.	66	14.	8	22.	24
6.	7	15.	48	23.	140
7.	110	16.	5	24.	11
8.	50	17.	36	25.	8
9.	7				

Section 2: mental calculation

For further guidance on efficient mental strategies, please see Chapter 2.

1.	132	9.	312
2.	588	10.	53
3.	16	11.	27,000
4.	37	12.	105
5.	216	13.	315
6.	145	14.	75
7.	56	15.	122
8.	115		

Section 3: informal pencil-and-paper calculation

For further guidance on possible approaches, please see Chapter 3.

1.	743	6.	642
2.	291	7.	19 remainder 12
3.	4458	8.	1282
4.	17	9.	19,616
5.	4888	10.	43 remainder 17

Section 4: traditional pencil-and-paper calculation

For further guidance on using the traditional compact methods, please see Chapter 4.

1.	882	6.	2051
2.	449	7.	21,369
3.	38,457	8.	208 remainder 6
4.	85 remainder 3	9.	113,183
5.	1554	10.	109 remainder 5

Section 5: calculation with fractions

For further guidance on working with fractions, please see Chapter 5.

1. $\dfrac{8}{12} = \dfrac{2}{3}$

2. $\dfrac{7}{12}$ is the smallest.

3. $\dfrac{3}{4}$ is the biggest.

4. $\dfrac{3}{4} + \dfrac{2}{3} = 1\dfrac{5}{12}$

5. $\dfrac{5}{8} - \dfrac{7}{12} = \dfrac{1}{24}$

6. $\dfrac{3}{4} \times \dfrac{2}{3} = \dfrac{1}{2}$

7. $\dfrac{3}{4} \div 2 = \dfrac{3}{8}$

8. £93.75

9. $\dfrac{2}{5}$

10. $1\dfrac{3}{4} \times 5 = 8\dfrac{3}{4}$ pints

Section 6: calculation with decimals

For further guidance on working with decimals, please see Chapter 5.

1. 3.089 is the smallest.

2. 3.105 is the biggest.

3. 3.089 and 3.09 are closest to one another.

4. 3.09 and 3.1 have a difference of one-hundredth $\left(\dfrac{1}{100}\right)$.

5. $3.089 + 3.09 = 6.179$

6. $3.105 - 3.089 = 0.016$

7. $3.089 \times 7 = 21.623$

8. $3.09 \times 3.1 = 9.579$

9. $3.089 \div 2 = 1.5445$

10. $3.105 \div 3 = 1.035$

Section 7: calculation with percentages

For further guidance on working with percentages, please see Chapter 5.

1. 76%

2. 45%

3. 62.5%

4. £75

5. £105

6. £101.25

7. £51

8. £35

Section 8: calculation with ratios

For further guidance on working with ratios, please see Chapter 5.

1. 1:4

2. 2:3

3. 30%

4. 35 kg sand.

5. 150 g of flour and 60 g of sugar.

6. 250 g of flour and 100 g of sugar.

Section 9: calculation with a calculator

For further guidance on using a calculator, please see Chapter 6.

1. $28^2 + 29^2 + 30^2 + 31^2 = 3486$

2. 12.247

3. 15.33

4. 5.56

5. 25.623

6. 10 years.